INFOGRAPHIC

GUIDE TO THE

MOVIES

An Hachette UK Company
www.hachette.co.uk

First published in Great Britain in 2013 by
Cassell Illustrated, a division of Octopus Publishing Group Ltd

Endeavour House
189 Shaftesbury Avenue
London
WC2H 8JY

www.octopusbooks.co.uk

ISBN 978-1-844037-52-0

A CIP catalogue record for this book is available from the British Library

Printed and bound in China

1 3 5 7 9 10 8 6 4 2

INFOGRAPHIC

GUIDE TO THE

MOVIES

KAREN KRIZANOVICH

CASSELL
ILLUSTRATED

CONTENTS

Introduction

by Karen Krizanovich

Even though few (and fewer) people are professional critics, everyone thinks they are movie critics, and there are good reasons for this. As Alfred Hitchcock said, 'Drama is life with the dull parts left out,' and we love films because they allow an escape from ordinary life and lead us to see new possibilities in our own existence. They show us things we haven't even imagined, like who'd have thought a basketball could be your best friend (as in *Cast Away*)?

What Hitchcock said about life also applies to infographics: they represent statistical information with all the boring stuff left out. Experts say that infographics are often the fastest and most memorable way to grasp the facts. This is because infographics slot right into our visual system's tendency to look for patterns and trends, allowing brains (and their owners) to stash vital information and keep it fresh. In short, when you learn something via an infographic, the practical result is that you'll probably do better at a party, quiz or job interview. Infographics, if used wisely, could make you a popular source of knowledge. Or a wiseass, which would be bad, so take care when using this stuff in public.

Everyone thinks they know more about films than they really do. You don't get people arguing over modern dance or classical bluegrass music the way people go on and on about films. Just because you spend large parts of your life watching films does not make you an expert, however. Hence, in the competitive sphere of 'talking about films', film infographics give you a keen overview of vital arguments about zombies, James Bond locations and so much more. Such knowledge will undoubtedly astound and edify those who weren't quite sure what to make of you. Also, for those who are not numerically inclined, infographics can provide a historical timeline that's easy to remember. In an art form such as films – which are also a popular entertainment – visual mnemonics are key to building a frame for serious thinking.

Naturally, infographics can't cover everything, even when they are as adorable and witty as these are. There will be items with which you will take exception—but remember what the famous statistician George E. P. Box said in 1987; 'Essentially, all models are wrong, but some are useful.' Infographics are useful but they are not and cannot be the whole story. This is because even the whole story is never the whole story in the unending tramp towards the cinematic future, whatever that turns out to be (a quick 'Hello!' to the inventors of the Betamax). As the famous American mathematician John Tukey also quipped, 'Far better an approximate answer to the right question, which is often vague, than an exact answer to the wrong question, which can always be made precise.' I'd say to Mr Tukey, 'Attaboy!' if only I knew him personally.

Enjoy an infographic and marvel at the cleverness of its visuals and the sheer variety of the ways in which it covers data that you think you know. And if you find something that is reasonably wrong–this means sticking to the same level of detail the graphic has and not going further into the Morass of More Data–well done! There's always more data being found, and this changes the way we look at old data. The two need each other. Without the data appreciater, all graphics would be for nought. Or, as H. G. Wells wrote in 1904, 'The time may not be very remote when it will be understood that for complete initiation as an efficient citizen of one of the new great complex world wide states that are now developing, it is as necessary to be able to compute, to think in averages and maxima and minima, as it is now to be able to read and write.' Infographics are, perhaps, essential training for your future.

There will be things that we've left out on purpose, and you want to know why? Because as the great actor, director, producer and movie sage Sean Penn once said; 'When everything gets answered, it's fake.'

MAY TO DECEMBER **AFFAIRS**

The age difference between male and female leads in movies has often been a story of May–December romances, and things have barely changed since 1946 when Bogey – who was almost 30 years older than his co-star – wooed and won Lauren Bacall. In 2011, Liam Neeson was 26 years older than his wife in Unknown, *January Jones. But then, in 2010 Melissa Leo (50) played mother to Mark Wahlberg (39) in* The Fighter...

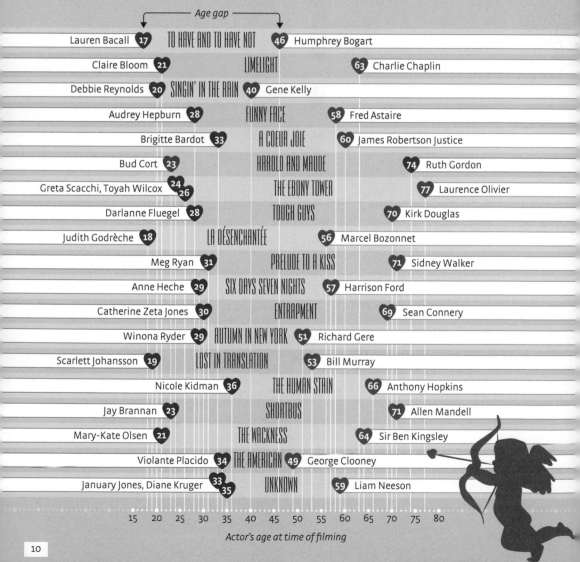

Age gap

Female lead	Film	Male lead
Lauren Bacall **17**	TO HAVE AND TO HAVE NOT	**46** Humphrey Bogart
Claire Bloom **21**	LIMELIGHT	**63** Charlie Chaplin
Debbie Reynolds **20**	SINGIN' IN THE RAIN	**40** Gene Kelly
Audrey Hepburn **28**	FUNNY FACE	**58** Fred Astaire
Brigitte Bardot **33**	A COEUR JOIE	**60** James Robertson Justice
Bud Cort **23**	HAROLD AND MAUDE	**74** Ruth Gordon
Greta Scacchi, Toyah Wilcox **24 26**	THE EBONY TOWER	**77** Laurence Olivier
Darlanne Fluegel **28**	TOUGH GUYS	**70** Kirk Douglas
Judith Godrèche **18**	LA DÉSENCHANTÉE	**56** Marcel Bozonnet
Meg Ryan **31**	PRELUDE TO A KISS	**71** Sidney Walker
Anne Heche **29**	SIX DAYS SEVEN NIGHTS	**57** Harrison Ford
Catherine Zeta Jones **30**	ENTRAPMENT	**69** Sean Connery
Winona Ryder **29**	AUTUMN IN NEW YORK	**51** Richard Gere
Scarlett Johansson **19**	LOST IN TRANSLATION	**53** Bill Murray
Nicole Kidman **36**	THE HUMAN STAIN	**66** Anthony Hopkins
Jay Brannan **23**	SHORTBUS	**71** Allen Mandell
Mary-Kate Olsen **21**	THE WACKNESS	**64** Sir Ben Kingsley
Violante Placido **34**	THE AMERICAN **49** George Clooney	
January Jones, Diane Kruger **33 35**	UNKNOWN	**59** Liam Neeson

15 20 25 30 35 40 45 50 55 60 65 70 75 80

Actor's age at time of filming

URBAN MYTHS: **THE MOVIES**

Urban myths have been handed down the generations since a trip to the movies meant watching shadows flicker on a cave wall. Naturally those myths have become the stuff of major (and minor) movie plots.

Bloody Mary – looking in a mirror and chanting a spirit's name can call them into being
Beetlejuice, Candyman, Bloody Mary, The Legend Of Bloody Mary, Paranormal Activity 3

Aliens have left 'signs' for us to read on Earth
Stargate (pyramids), The Fifth Element (pyramids), Signs (crop circles), Alien Vs. Predator (2004, Pyramid)

Bigfoot, a large, unidentified ape-like creature covered in brown hair walks the mountains and forests of North America
Bigfoot, The Legend Of Boggy Creek, Night Of The Demon, Harry And The Hendersons, Monsters, Inc., Abominable, Strange Wilderness

Men in black suits who claim to be investigating UFO sightings for the government are actually aliens, or at least half-aliens
Invasion Of The Body Snatchers, Men In Black (1997), The Matrix (1999), Men In Black II (2002), The Matrix Revolutions (2003), The Matrix Reloaded (2003), MIB 3 (2012)

The Hook, in which an escaped lunatic with a hook for a hand leaves it hanging from a young couple's make-out vehicle
I Know What You Did Last Summer, I Still Know What You Did Last Summer, Lovers Lane, I'll Always Know What You Did Last Summer

The Babysitter and the Killer Upstairs, in which a female babysitter receives frightening phone calls while babysitting... that are coming from the house in which she's sitting
Fright, Black Christmas, Halloween, When A Stranger Calls, When A Stranger Calls Back, Scream, The House Of The Devil

NAME THAT MOVIE **1970S**

Use these graphics to identify the titles of ten memorable films from the 1970s. The first letter of each film title is included to help you identify it.

HAVE YOU SEEN THIS WOMAN?

The composite perfect leading lady according to a panel of (female) critics would look like this:

Cameron Diaz's eyes
There's Something About Mary, 1998
$370m

Natalie Portman's nose
Star Wars Episode I – The Phantom Menace, 1999
$1.03bn

Angelina Jolie's lips
Mr & Mrs Smith, 2005
$478m

Halle Berry's neck
X-Men: The Last Stand, 2006
$459m

Milla Jovovich's arms
The Fifth Element, 1997
$264m

Keira Knightley's hips
Pirates Of The Caribbean: Dead Man's Chest, 2006
$1.07bn

Geena Davis' skull [and Susan Sarandon's brain]
Thelma & Louise, 1991
$100m

Megan Fox's hair
Transformers: Revenge Of The Fallen, 2009
$836m

Kate Blanchett's cheekbones
Lord Of The Rings: Return Of The King, 2003
$1.12bn

Anne Hathaway's chin
The Dark Knight Rises, 2012
$1.1bn

Scarlett Johansson's breasts
Marvel's The Avengers, 2012
$1.5bn

Kate Beckinsale's rear end
Pearl Harbor, 2001
$449m

Olivia Wilde's legs
Tron Legacy, 2010
$400m

HOLLYWOOD'S **MOST** WANTED (PART 1)

The top six actors in terms of career box office success in America are, in decreasing order, Tom Hanks, Eddie Murphy, Harrison Ford, Samuel L. Jackson, Morgan Freeman and Tom Cruise. Plotting the route of their success over each actor's career throws up some interesting facts.

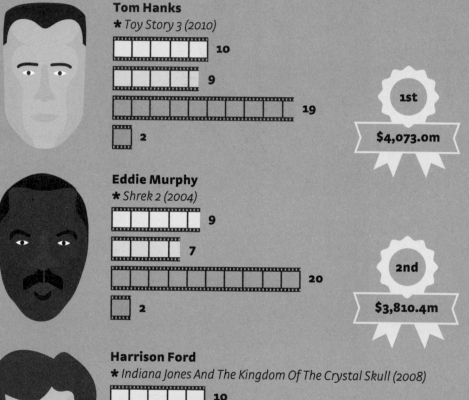

Tom Hanks
* *Toy Story 3 (2010)*

10

9

19

2

1st

$4,073.0m

Eddie Murphy
* *Shrek 2 (2004)*

9

7

20

2

2nd

$3,810.4m

Harrison Ford
* *Indiana Jones And The Kingdom Of The Crystal Skull (2008)*

10

8

13

3

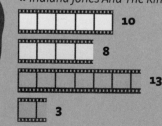

3rd

$3,561.6m

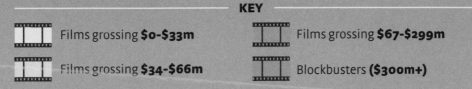

KEY

	Films grossing **$0-$33m**		Films grossing **$67-$299m**
	Films grossing **$34-$66m**		Blockbusters **($300m+)**

* = highest grossing film

Samuel L. Jackson
* *Marvel's The Avengers (2012)*

34

13

7

4

4th

$3,504.9m

Morgan Freeman
* *The Dark Knight (2008)*

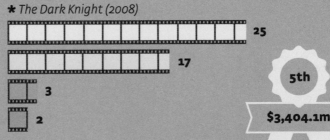

25

17

3

2

5th

$3,404.1m

Tom Cruise
* *War Of The Worlds (2005)*

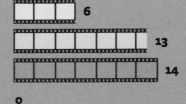

6

13

14

0

6th

$3,164.4m

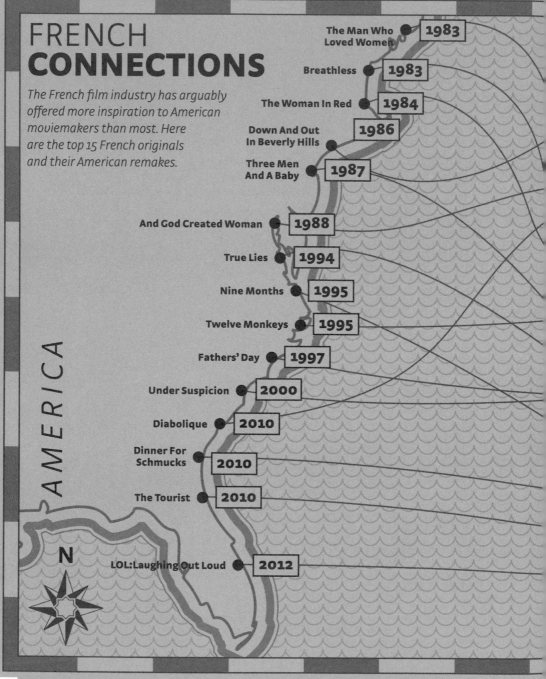

FRENCH
CONNECTIONS

The French film industry has arguably offered more inspiration to American moviemakers than most. Here are the top 15 French originals and their American remakes.

The Man Who Loved Women — 1983
Breathless — 1983
The Woman In Red — 1984
Down And Out In Beverly Hills — 1986
Three Men And A Baby — 1987
And God Created Woman — 1988
True Lies — 1994
Nine Months — 1995
Twelve Monkeys — 1995
Fathers' Day — 1997
Under Suspicion — 2000
Diabolique — 2010
Dinner For Schmucks — 2010
The Tourist — 2010
LOL: Laughing Out Loud — 2012

AMERICA

N

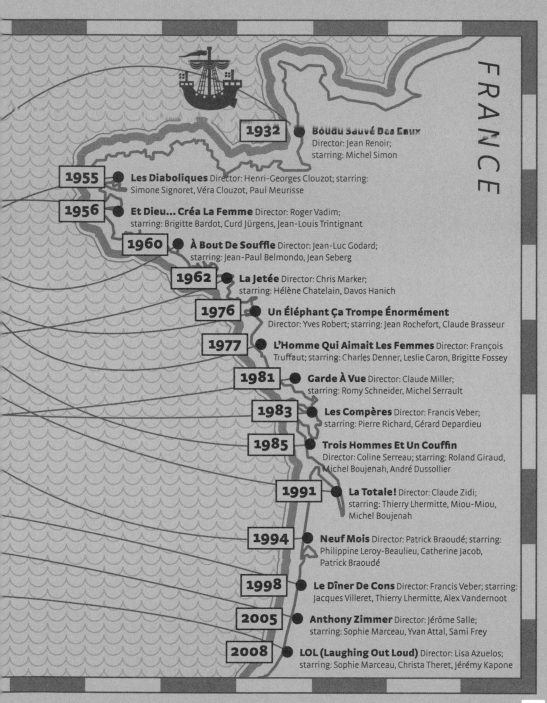

1932 Boudu Sauvé Des Eaux
Director: Jean Renoir;
starring: Michel Simon

1955 **Les Diaboliques** Director: Henri-Georges Clouzot; starring:
Simone Signoret, Véra Clouzot, Paul Meurisse

1956 **Et Dieu... Créa La Femme** Director: Roger Vadim;
starring: Brigitte Bardot, Curd Jürgens, Jean-Louis Trintignant

1960 **À Bout De Souffle** Director: Jean-Luc Godard;
starring: Jean-Paul Belmondo, Jean Seberg

1962 **La Jetée** Director: Chris Marker;
starring: Hélène Chatelain, Davos Hanich

1976 **Un Éléphant Ça Trompe Énormément**
Director: Yves Robert; starring: Jean Rochefort, Claude Brasseur

1977 **L'Homme Qui Aimait Les Femmes** Director: François
Truffaut; starring: Charles Denner, Leslie Caron, Brigitte Fossey

1981 **Garde À Vue** Director: Claude Miller;
starring: Romy Schneider, Michel Serrault

1983 **Les Compères** Director: Francis Veber;
starring: Pierre Richard, Gérard Depardieu

1985 **Trois Hommes Et Un Couffin**
Director: Coline Serreau; starring: Roland Giraud,
Michel Boujenah, André Dussollier

1991 **La Totale!** Director: Claude Zidi;
starring: Thierry Lhermitte, Miou-Miou,
Michel Boujenah

1994 **Neuf Mois** Director: Patrick Braoudé; starring:
Philippine Leroy-Beaulieu, Catherine Jacob,
Patrick Braoudé

1998 **Le Dîner De Cons** Director: Francis Veber; starring:
Jacques Villeret, Thierry Lhermitte, Alex Vandernoot

2005 **Anthony Zimmer** Director: Jérôme Salle;
starring: Sophie Marceau, Yvan Attal, Sami Frey

2008 **LOL (Laughing Out Loud)** Director: Lisa Azuelos;
starring: Sophie Marceau, Christa Theret, Jérémy Kapone

KUNG FU **KING**

Who is Kung Fu King – Jackie Chan or Jet Li? Based on the box office success of each fighter's most successful movies, then Jet Li (b. Bejing, China, 4/26/63) has outfought his sometime co-star Jackie Chan (b. Hong Kong, 4/7/1954) to take more money at cinemas around the world.

Jet Li's Fearless
(2006)
Worldwide gross
$68,072,848

Top 3 grossing movies
Lethal Weapon 4 [1998]
The Expendables [2010]
The Mummy: Tomb of the Emperor [2008]
Total worldwide gross
$961,043,636

JET LI

The Expendables 1 & 2
(2010, '12)
Worldwide gross
$574,898,586

Hero (2004)
Worldwide gross
$177,394,432

TOGETHER
Jackie Chan & Jet Li

THE GHOST OF KUNG FU PAST: BRUCE LEE

Unfortunately accurate box office figures for the three most successful movies made by Kung Fu legend Bruce Lee (b. San Francisco, USA, 11/27/40, d. Kowloon, HK, 7/20/1973) are not available, but an estimate (via imbd.com) puts them at a combined $320,000,000.

Shanghai Knights
(2003)
Worldwide gross
$88,323,487

Jackie Chan's
First Strike
(1997)
Worldwide gross
$21,890,845

Top 3 grossing movies
Rush Hour 2 [2001]
Karate Kid [2010]
Rush Hour [1998]
Total worldwide gross
$950,838,688

JACKIE CHAN

The Forbidden Kingdom (2008)
Worldwide gross **$127,980,002**

*The Rush Hour
Series*
(1998, '01, '07)
Total gross
$507,477,118

| 1 | *Fist of Fury* (1972) estimated worldwide gross **$100,000,000** | 2 | *Enter The Dragon* (1973) estimated worldwide gross **$90,000,000** | 3 | *Way Of The Dragon* (1972) estimated worldwide gross **$130,000** |

THROUGH THE **MATRIX**

*Track Neo's route through the first Matrix movie by following the scenes below
from 1–20, which show the key interactions in three zones of existence.*

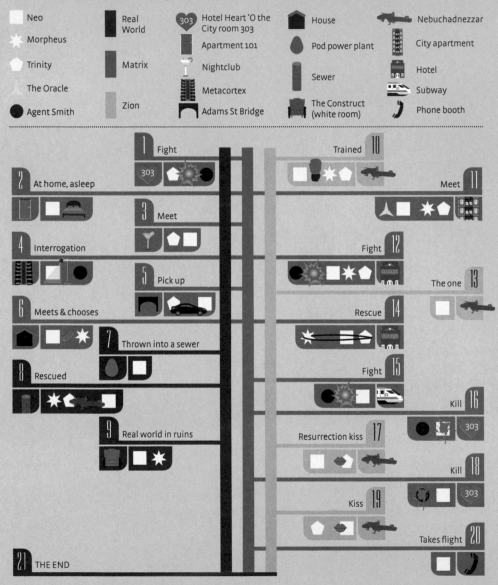

Neo

Morpheus

Trinity

The Oracle

Agent Smith

Real World

Matrix

Zion

303 Hotel Heart 'O the City room 303

Apartment 101

Nightclub

Metacortex

Adams St Bridge

House

Pod power plant

Sewer

The Construct (white room)

Nebuchadnezzar

City apartment

Hotel

Subway

Phone booth

1 Fight

2 At home, asleep

3 Meet

4 Interrogation

5 Pick up

6 Meets & chooses

7 Thrown into a sewer

8 Rescued

9 Real world in ruins

10 Trained

11 Meet

12 Fight

13 The one

14 Rescue

15 Fight

16 Kill

17 Resurrection kiss

18 Kill

19 Kiss

20 Takes flight

21 THE END

'I'M REALLY AN ACTOR...'

Even Hollywood movie stars had day jobs while they were trying to make it. Here are the jobs and wages that 9 stars would be earning if they had stayed in those jobs, compared with their earnings since getting the big break...

* Average Wage for a 40-Hour Work Week

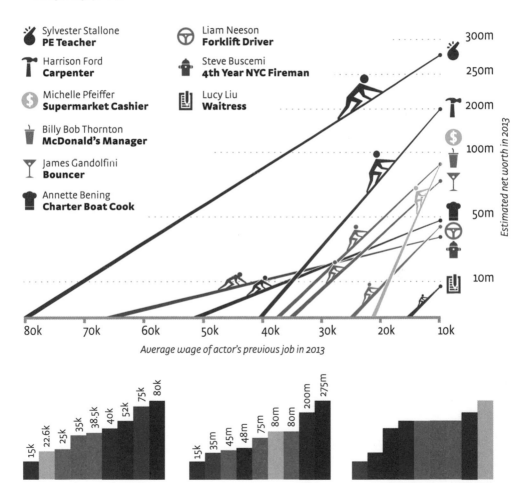

Sylvester Stallone
PE Teacher

Liam Neeson
Forklift Driver

Harrison Ford
Carpenter

Steve Buscemi
4th Year NYC Fireman

Michelle Pfeiffer
Supermarket Cashier

Lucy Liu
Waitress

Billy Bob Thornton
McDonald's Manager

James Gandolfini
Bouncer

Annette Bening
Charter Boat Cook

Estimated net worth in 2013

300m
250m
200m
100m
50m
10m

80k   70k   60k   50k   40k   30k   20k   10k

Average wage of actor's previous job in 2013

Original Earnings: 15k, 22.6k, 25k, 35k, 38.5k, 40k, 52k, 75k, 80k

Movie Actor Earnings: 15k, 35m, 45m, 48m, 75m, 80m, 80m, 200m, 275m

Steepness of Increase

ON LOCATION: **EUROPE**

Since the millennium, European countries have offered tax break incentives for filmmakers to use their territories for shoots. These cities have presented themselves as the perfect place to make certain kinds of films, as shown by these prime examples of different genre style cinema.

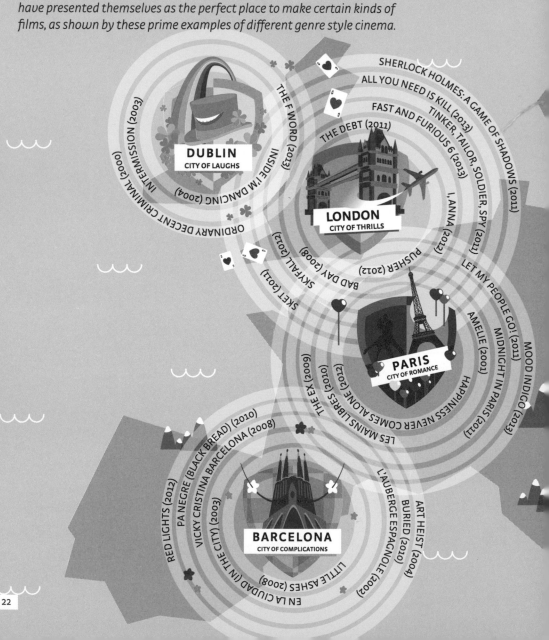

DUBLIN
CITY OF LAUGHS

INTERMISSION (2000)
ORDINARY DECENT CRIMINAL (2000)
INSIDE I'M DANCING (2004)
THE F WORD (2013)

LONDON
CITY OF THRILLS

THE DEBT (2011)
SHERLOCK HOLMES: A GAME OF SHADOWS (2011)
ALL YOU NEED IS KILL (2013)
TINKER, TAILOR, SOLDIER, SPY (2011)
FAST AND FURIOUS 6 (2013)
I, ANNA (2012)
LET MY PEOPLE GO! (2011)
PUSHER (2012)
BAD DAY (2008)
SKYFALL (2012)
SKET (2011)

PARIS
CITY OF ROMANCE

MOOD INDIGO (2013)
MIDNIGHT IN PARIS (2011)
AMELIE (2001)
HAPPINESS NEVER COMES ALONE (2012)
LES MAINS LIBRES (2010)
THE EX (2009)

BARCELONA
CITY OF COMPLICATIONS

RED LIGHTS (2012)
PA NEGRE (BLACK BREAD) (2010)
VICKY CRISTINA BARCELONA (2008)
EN LA CIUDAD (IN THE CITY) (2003)
LITTLE ASHES (2008)
L'AUBERGE ESPAGNOLE (2002)
BURIED (2010)
ART HEIST (2004)

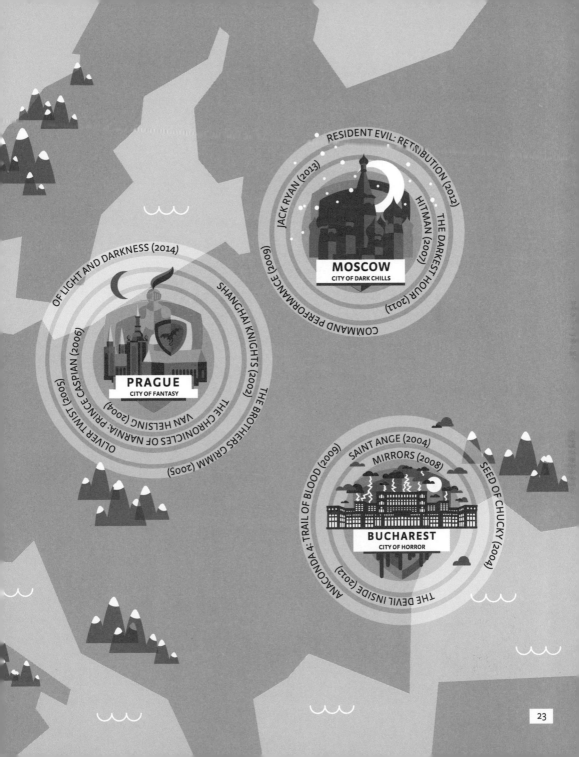

RESIDENT EVIL: RETRIBUTION (2012)

JACK RYAN (2013)

THE DARKEST HOUR (2011)

HITMAN (2007)

MOSCOW
CITY OF DARK CHILLS

COMMAND PERFORMANCE (2009)

OF LIGHT AND DARKNESS (2014)

SHANGHAI KNIGHTS (2002)

OLIVER TWIST (2005)

THE CHRONICLES OF NARNIA: PRINCE CASPIAN (2006)

VAN HELSING (2004)

THE BROTHERS GRIMM (2005)

PRAGUE
CITY OF FANTASY

SAINT ANGE (2004)

TRAIL OF BLOOD (2009)

MIRRORS (2008)

SEED OF CHUCKY (2004)

ANACONDA 4: TRAIL OF BLOOD (2009)

THE DEVIL INSIDE (2012)

BUCHAREST
CITY OF HORROR

THE OUTER LIMITS OF **KEVIN BACON**

How, in just six moves or less, Kevin Bacon can be connected with Abraham Lincoln, Queen Elizabeth II, Albert Einstein, Marshall McLuhan, Ingmar Bergman... and a dog named Moose.

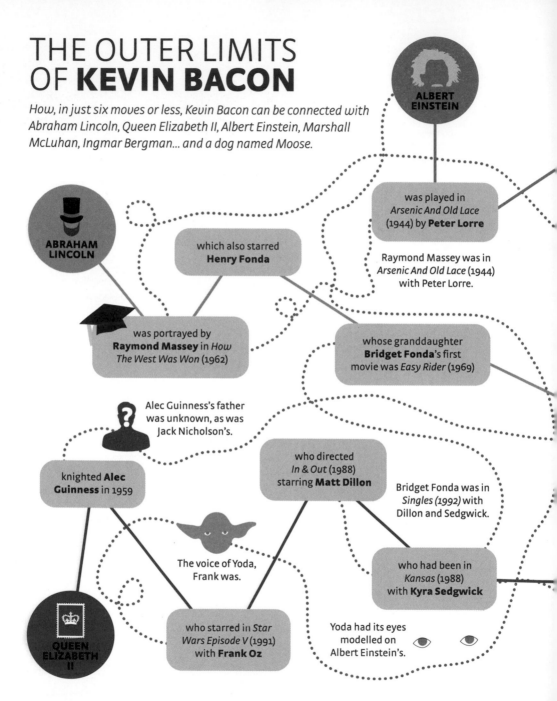

ALBERT EINSTEIN

ABRAHAM LINCOLN

which also starred **Henry Fonda**

was played in *Arsenic And Old Lace* (1944) by **Peter Lorre**

Raymond Massey was in *Arsenic And Old Lace* (1944) with Peter Lorre.

was portrayed by **Raymond Massey** in *How The West Was Won* (1962)

whose granddaughter **Bridget Fonda**'s first movie was *Easy Rider* (1969)

Alec Guinness's father was unknown, as was Jack Nicholson's.

knighted **Alec Guinness** in 1959

who directed *In & Out* (1988) starring **Matt Dillon**

Bridget Fonda was in *Singles* (1992) with Dillon and Sedgwick.

The voice of Yoda, Frank was.

who had been in *Kansas* (1988) with **Kyra Sedgwick**

QUEEN ELIZABETH II

who starred in *Star Wars Episode V* (1991) with **Frank Oz**

Yoda had its eyes modelled on Albert Einstein's.

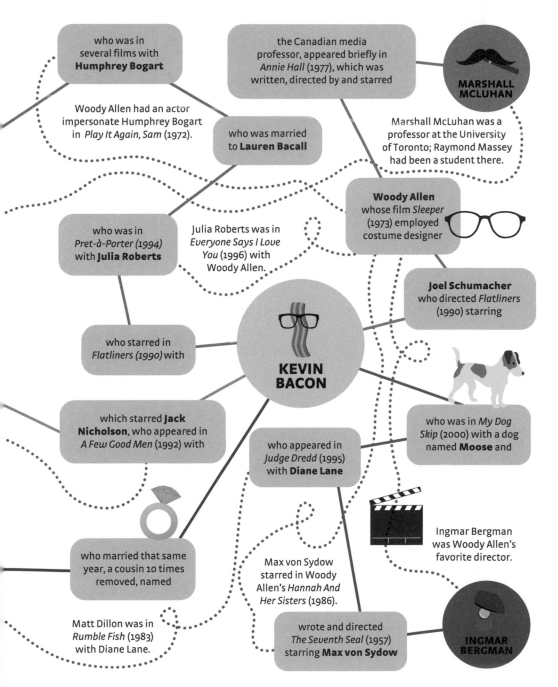

who was in several films with **Humphrey Bogart**

the Canadian media professor, appeared briefly in *Annie Hall* (1977), which was written, directed by and starred

MARSHALL McLUHAN

Woody Allen had an actor impersonate Humphrey Bogart in *Play It Again, Sam* (1972).

who was married to **Lauren Bacall**

Marshall McLuhan was a professor at the University of Toronto; Raymond Massey had been a student there.

who was in *Pret-à-Porter* (1994) with **Julia Roberts**

Julia Roberts was in *Everyone Says I Love You* (1996) with Woody Allen.

Woody Allen whose film *Sleeper* (1973) employed costume designer

Joel Schumacher who directed *Flatliners* (1990) starring

who starred in *Flatliners (1990)* with

KEVIN BACON

which starred **Jack Nicholson**, who appeared in *A Few Good Men* (1992) with

who appeared in *Judge Dredd* (1995) with **Diane Lane**

who was in *My Dog Skip* (2000) with a dog named **Moose** and

Ingmar Bergman was Woody Allen's favorite director.

who married that same year, a cousin 10 times removed, named

Max von Sydow starred in Woody Allen's *Hannah And Her Sisters* (1986).

Matt Dillon was in *Rumble Fish* (1983) with Diane Lane.

wrote and directed *The Seventh Seal* (1957) starring **Max von Sydow**

INGMAR BERGMAN

LEVELS OF
INCEPTION

*Follow the journeys of the characters in the movie
as they move through the four levels of dream
times while asleep on a flight from Sydney to Los
Angeles. Each line represents a different character's
time spent at different levels of dream state.*

SYD

1

2

LI

LAX

TEMPORAL CHANGES IN LEVELS OF DREAM

	Reality	**1**	Seconds
Level 1	**Van**	**20**	Seconds
Level 2	**Hotel**	**6**	Minutes
Level 3	**Fortress**	**2**	Hours
Level 4	**Dream City**	**40**	Hours
	Limbo	**33**	Days

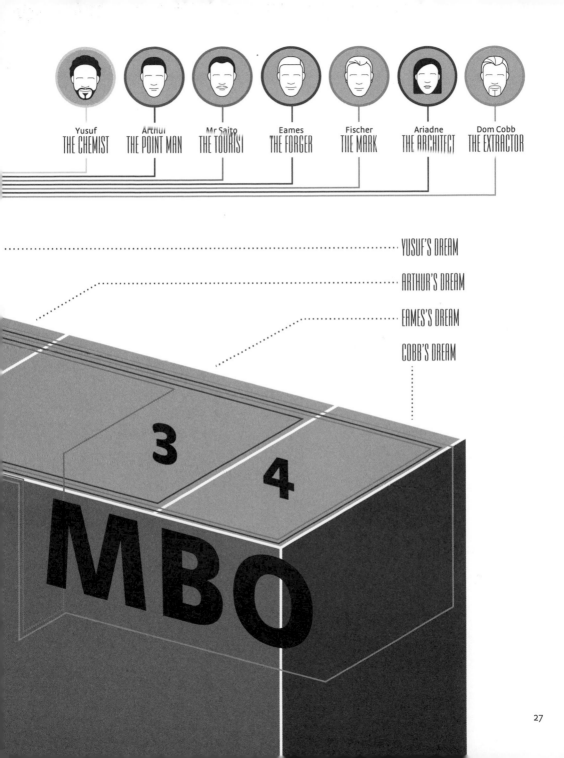

Yusuf
THE CHEMIST

Arthur
THE POINT MAN

Mr Saito
THE TOURIST

Eames
THE FORGER

Fischer
THE MARK

Ariadne
THE ARCHITECT

Dom Cobb
THE EXTRACTOR

YUSUF'S DREAM

ARTHUR'S DREAM

EAMES'S DREAM

COBB'S DREAM

3

4

MBO

MISSING THE
LAST MOVIE
SHOW

The most successful young (under 40 when they died) actors rated by the box office of their final movie

Heath
LEDGER

4/4/79 – 1/22/08 (28)

The Imaginarium Of Dr Parnassus
December 2009
£61.8m

AALIYAH

1/16/79 – 8/25/01 (22)

Queen Of The Damned
Feb 2002
£45.5m

JAMES DEAN

2/8/31 – 9/30/55 (24)

Giant
October 1956
£35m

Marilyn
MONROE

6/1/26 – 8/5/62 (36)

The Misfits
January 1961

£8.2m

Chris
FARLEY

2/15/64 – 12/18/97 (33)

Almost Heroes
May 1998

£6.137m

Carole
LOMBARD

10/6/08 – 1/16/42 (33)

To Be Or Not To Be
March 1942

£2.1m

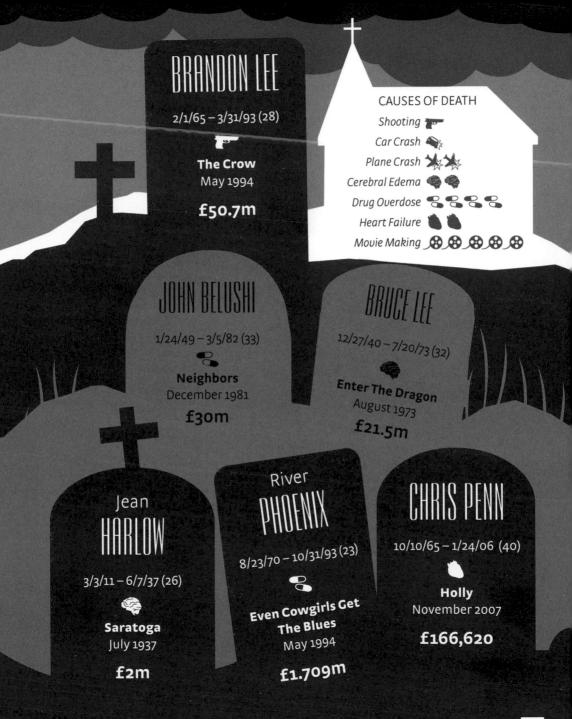

BRANDON LEE

2/1/65 – 3/31/93 (28)

The Crow
May 1994

£50.7m

CAUSES OF DEATH

Shooting
Car Crash
Plane Crash
Cerebral Edema
Drug Overdose
Heart Failure
Movie Making

JOHN BELUSHI

1/24/49 – 3/5/82 (33)

Neighbors
December 1981

£30m

BRUCE LEE

12/27/40 – 7/20/73 (32)

Enter The Dragon
August 1973

£21.5m

Jean HARLOW

3/3/11 – 6/7/37 (26)

Saratoga
July 1937

£2m

River PHOENIX

8/23/70 – 10/31/93 (23)

Even Cowgirls Get The Blues
May 1994

£1.709m

CHRIS PENN

10/10/65 – 1/24/06 (40)

Holly
November 2007

£166,620

I'M **ALAN SMITHEE**

The name of Alan Smithee is added to a movie as director when the actual director(s) doesn't want to be credited with the release. It's usually a smart move, rarely regretted by the real director.
Note that An Alan Smithee Film: Burn Hollywood Burn *(in which Eric Idle plays Smithee), cost around $10 million to make.*

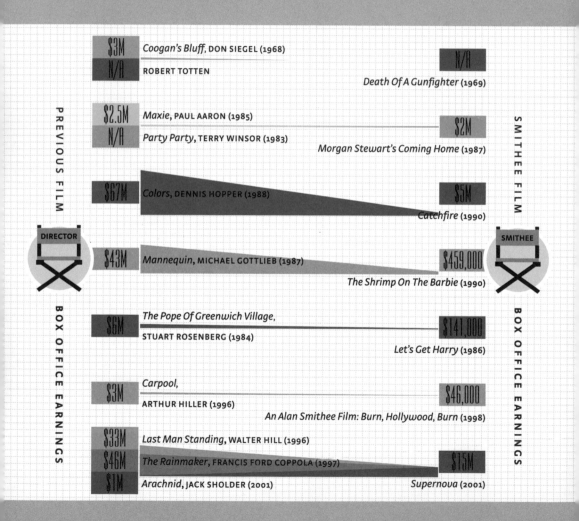

PREVIOUS FILM

SMITHEE FILM

DIRECTOR

SMITHEE

BOX OFFICE EARNINGS

BOX OFFICE EARNINGS

$3M — *Coogan's Bluff*, DON SIEGEL (1968)
N/A — ROBERT TOTTEN
N/A — *Death Of A Gunfighter* (1969)

$2.5M — *Maxie*, PAUL AARON (1985)
N/A — *Party Party*, TERRY WINSOR (1983)
$2M — *Morgan Stewart's Coming Home* (1987)

$67M — *Colors*, DENNIS HOPPER (1988)
$5M — *Catchfire* (1990)

$43M — *Mannequin*, MICHAEL GOTTLIEB (1987)
$459,000 — *The Shrimp On The Barbie* (1990)

$6M — *The Pope Of Greenwich Village*, STUART ROSENBERG (1984)
$141,000 — *Let's Get Harry* (1986)

$3M — *Carpool*, ARTHUR HILLER (1996)
$46,000 — *An Alan Smithee Film: Burn, Hollywood, Burn* (1998)

$33M — *Last Man Standing*, WALTER HILL (1996)
$46M — *The Rainmaker*, FRANCIS FORD COPPOLA (1997)
$1M — *Arachnid*, JACK SHOLDER (2001)
$15M — *Supernova* (2001)

 Information courtesy of Box Office Mojo and IMDb (http://www.imdb.com). Used with permission.

WHO IS RYAN GOSLING?

Early in 2013 Ryan Gosling (11/21/80) announced that he was taking a break from acting so that he could 'reassess why I'm doing it and how I'm doing it'. To help with the reassessment, here are his ten most successful movies, and the parts he acted in them.

ACTION
COMEDY
CRIME
DRAMA
ROMANTIC DRAMA
THRILLER

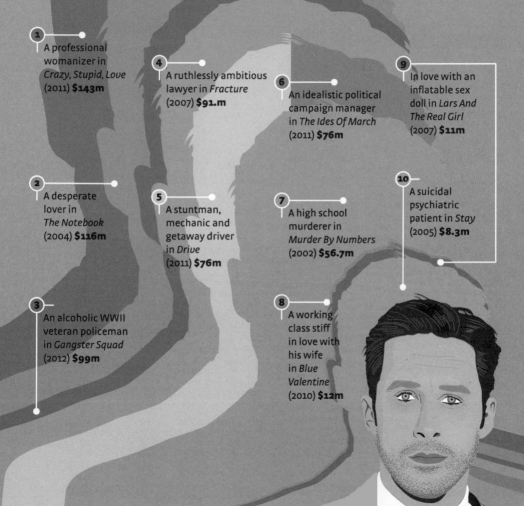

1 A professional womanizer in *Crazy, Stupid, Love* (2011) **$143m**

2 A desperate lover in *The Notebook* (2004) **$116m**

3 An alcoholic WWII veteran policeman in *Gangster Squad* (2012) **$99m**

4 A ruthlessly ambitious lawyer in *Fracture* (2007) **$91.m**

5 A stuntman, mechanic and getaway driver in *Drive* (2011) **$76m**

6 An idealistic political campaign manager in *The Ides Of March* (2011) **$76m**

7 A high school murderer in *Murder By Numbers* (2002) **$56.7m**

8 A working class stiff in love with his wife in *Blue Valentine* (2010) **$12m**

9 In love with an inflatable sex doll in *Lars And The Real Girl* (2007) **$11m**

10 A suicidal psychiatric patient in *Stay* (2005) **$8.3m**

MORE **BANG** FOR **BUCKS**

It takes a lot of bucks to make movies filled with bangs. Here are the costs for explosions, cars and 'copters for five top grossing action stars' key movies.

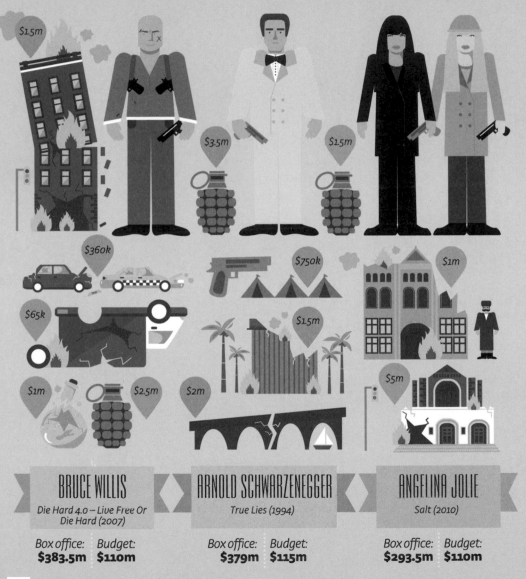

$1.5m

$3.5m

$1.5m

$360k

$750k

$1m

$65k

$1.5m

$1m

$2.5m

$2m

$5m

BRUCE WILLIS	ARNOLD SCHWARZENEGGER	ANGELINA JOLIE
Die Hard 4.0 – Live Free Or Die Hard (2007)	True Lies (1994)	Salt (2010)

Box office:	Budget:	Box office:	Budget:	Box office:	Budget:
$383.5m	**$110m**	**$379m**	**$115m**	**$293.5m**	**$110m**

$3.7m

= cost   = helicopters

= explosions   = tech items

= automobiles   = destruction
                  of buildings

= armoured
  vehicles

$6m $1m

$500m

$345k

$1.5m $1.5m

SYLVESTER STALLONE   MEL GIBSON
The Expendables (2010)   Lethal Weapon 2 (1989)

Box office : Budget: Box office : Budget:
$274.5m $80m $228m $25m

F

T

U

Z

L

D

NAME THAT
MOVIE 1980S

*Use these graphics to identify the titles of ten
memorable films from the 1980s. The first letter
of each film title is included to help you identify it.*

X

B

P

THE GREAT **ROM-COM** AFFAIR

The perfect cast to make the most successful rom-com in movie history would be...

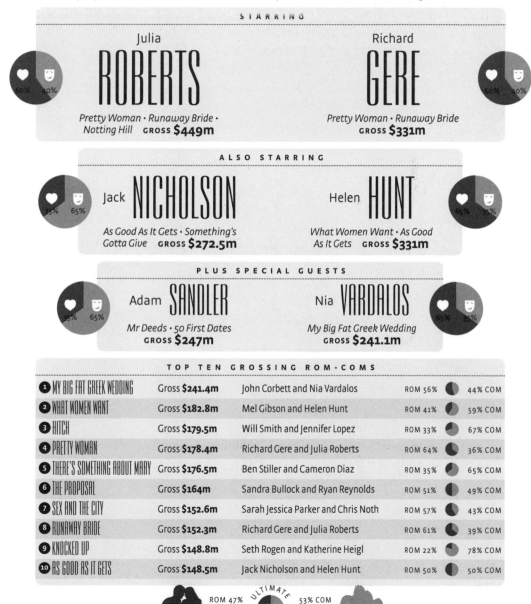

STARRING

Julia
ROBERTS

60% 40%

Pretty Woman · Runaway Bride ·
Notting Hill GROSS **$449m**

Richard
GERE

60% 40%

Pretty Woman · Runaway Bride
GROSS **$331m**

ALSO STARRING

Jack NICHOLSON

35% 65%

As Good As It Gets · Something's
Gotta Give GROSS **$272.5m**

Helen HUNT

65% 35%

What Women Want · As Good
As It Gets GROSS **$331m**

PLUS SPECIAL GUESTS

Adam SANDLER

35% 65%

Mr Deeds · 50 First Dates
GROSS **$247m**

Nia VARDALOS

65% 35%

My Big Fat Greek Wedding
GROSS **$241.1m**

TOP TEN GROSSING ROM-COMS

#	Title	Gross	Stars	ROM	COM
1	MY BIG FAT GREEK WEDDING	Gross $241.4m	John Corbett and Nia Vardalos	ROM 56%	44% COM
2	WHAT WOMEN WANT	Gross $182.8m	Mel Gibson and Helen Hunt	ROM 41%	59% COM
3	HITCH	Gross $179.5m	Will Smith and Jennifer Lopez	ROM 33%	67% COM
4	PRETTY WOMAN	Gross $178.4m	Richard Gere and Julia Roberts	ROM 64%	36% COM
5	THERE'S SOMETHING ABOUT MARY	Gross $176.5m	Ben Stiller and Cameron Diaz	ROM 35%	65% COM
6	THE PROPOSAL	Gross $164m	Sandra Bullock and Ryan Reynolds	ROM 51%	49% COM
7	SEX AND THE CITY	Gross $152.6m	Sarah Jessica Parker and Chris Noth	ROM 57%	43% COM
8	RUNAWAY BRIDE	Gross $152.3m	Richard Gere and Julia Roberts	ROM 61%	39% COM
9	KNOCKED UP	Gross $148.8m	Seth Rogen and Katherine Heigl	ROM 22%	78% COM
10	AS GOOD AS IT GETS	Gross $148.5m	Jack Nicholson and Helen Hunt	ROM 50%	50% COM

ROM 47% ULTIMATE 53% COM

Information courtesy of Box Office Mojo. Used with permission.
Additional information Karen Krizanovich

WHO'S THE BEST **BOND**?

Here we celebrate 50 years of James Bond by visualizing how many women each Bond has bedded, what gadgets he has debuted, how many Martinis he has quaffed. And most importantly, statistically speaking, was Connery really better than Moore?

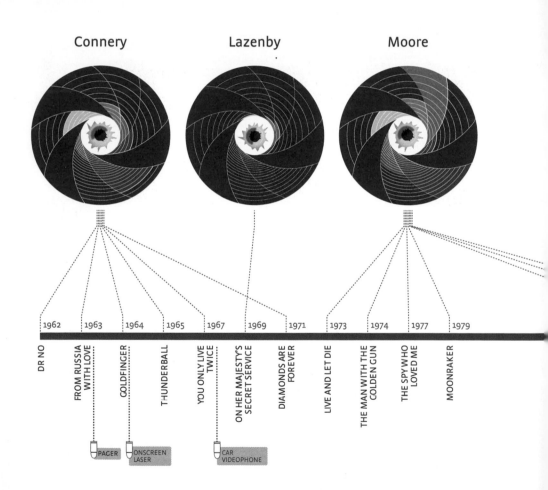

Connery   Lazenby   Moore

| 1962 | 1963 | 1964 | 1965 | 1967 | 1969 | 1971 | 1973 | 1974 | 1977 | 1979 |

DR NO

FROM RUSSIA WITH LOVE

GOLDFINGER

THUNDERBALL

YOU ONLY LIVE TWICE

ON HER MAJESTY'S SECRET SERVICE

DIAMONDS ARE FOREVER

LIVE AND LET DIE

THE MAN WITH THE GOLDEN GUN

THE SPY WHO LOVED ME

MOONRAKER

PAGER

ONSCREEN LASER

CAR VIDEOPHONE

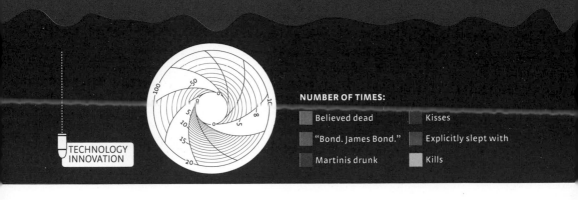

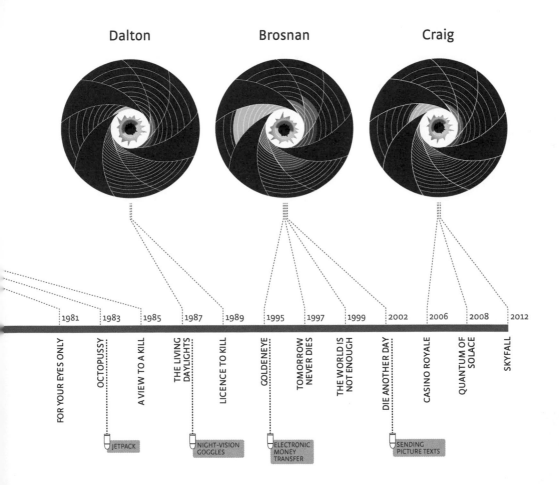

Dalton Brosnan Craig

FOR YOUR EYES ONLY
OCTOPUSSY
A VIEW TO A KILL
THE LIVING DAYLIGHTS
LICENCE TO KILL
GOLDENEYE
TOMORROW NEVER DIES
THE WORLD IS NOT ENOUGH
DIE ANOTHER DAY
CASINO ROYALE
QUANTUM OF SOLACE
SKYFALL

1981 1983 1985 1987 1989 1995 1997 1999 2002 2006 2008 2012

JETPACK
NIGHT-VISION GOGGLES
ELECTRONIC MONEY TRANSFER
SENDING PICTURE TEXTS

HOLY BOX OFFICE,
BATMAN!

Making a Batman movie is usually a way to increase an actor and director's box office appeal for future projects. These Batlights show the increase or decrease in average ticket sales for films made after Batman, compared to the average for films made before becoming or directing the caped crusader.

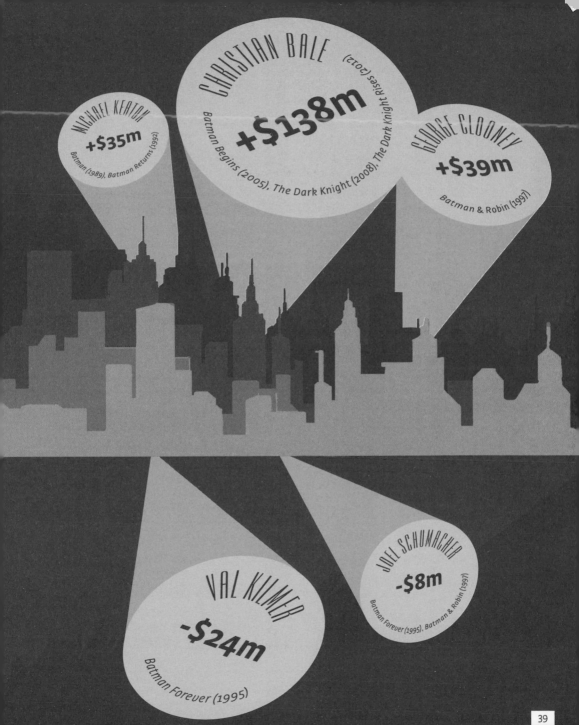

MICHAEL KEATON
+$35m
Batman (1989), Batman Returns (1992)

CHRISTIAN BALE
+$138m
Batman Begins (2005), The Dark Knight (2008), The Dark Knight Rises (2012)

GEORGE CLOONEY
+$39m
Batman & Robin (1997)

VAL KILMER
-$24m
Batman Forever (1995)

JOEL SCHUMACHER
-$8m
Batman Forever (1995), Batman & Robin (1997)

SWINGING
LONDON ON FILM

*These are the six most successful mid-1960s-made
movies and their route as they appear in sequence.*

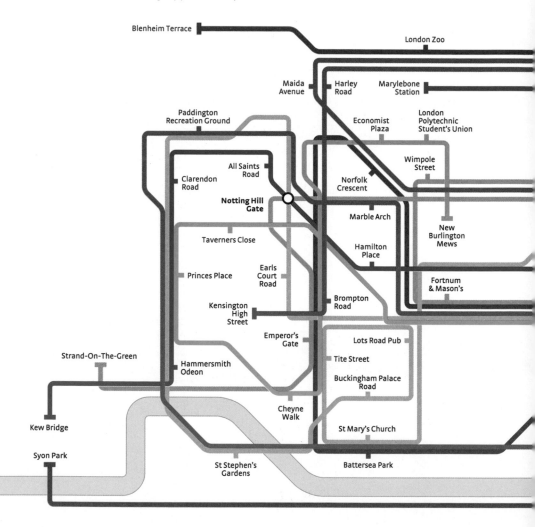

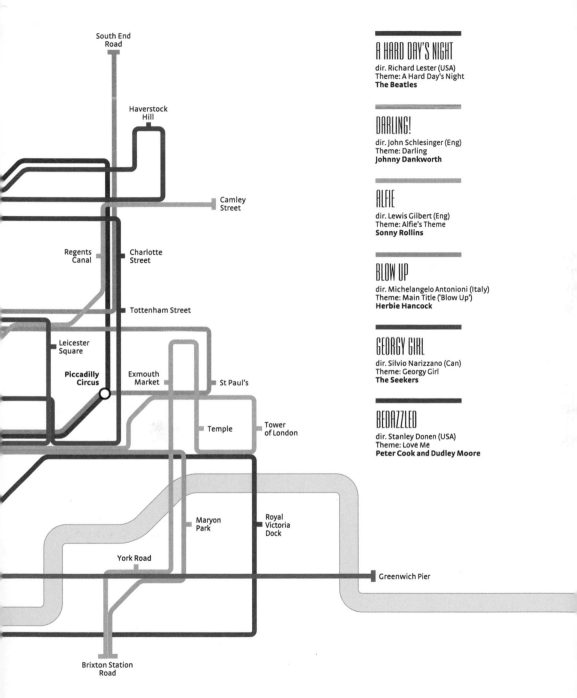

South End
Road

Haverstock
Hill

Camley
Street

Regents
Canal

Charlotte
Street

Tottenham Street

Leicester
Square

Exmouth
Market

St Paul's

**Piccadilly
Circus**

Temple

Tower
of London

Maryon
Park

Royal
Victoria
Dock

York Road

Greenwich Pier

Brixton Station
Road

A HARD DAY'S NIGHT

dir. Richard Lester (USA)
Theme: A Hard Day's Night
The Beatles

DARLING!

dir. John Schlesinger (Eng)
Theme: Darling
Johnny Dankworth

ALFIE

dir. Lewis Gilbert (Eng)
Theme: Alfie's Theme
Sonny Rollins

BLOW UP

dir. Michelangelo Antonioni (Italy)
Theme: Main Title ('Blow Up')
Herbie Hancock

GEORGY GIRL

dir. Silvio Narizzano (Can)
Theme: Georgy Girl
The Seekers

BEDAZZLED

dir. Stanley Donen (USA)
Theme: Love Me
Peter Cook and Dudley Moore

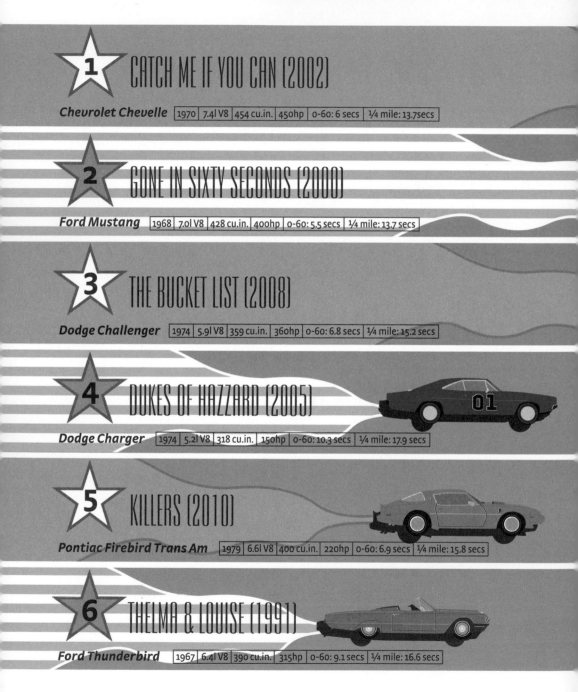

1 CATCH ME IF YOU CAN (2002)

Chevrolet Chevelle | 1970 | 7.4l V8 | 454 cu.in. | 450hp | 0-60: 6 secs | ¼ mile: 13.7secs

2 GONE IN SIXTY SECONDS (2000)

Ford Mustang | 1968 | 7.0l V8 | 428 cu.in. | 400hp | 0-60: 5.5 secs | ¼ mile: 13.7 secs

3 THE BUCKET LIST (2008)

Dodge Challenger | 1974 | 5.9l V8 | 359 cu.in. | 360hp | 0-60: 6.8 secs | ¼ mile: 15.2 secs

4 DUKES OF HAZZARD (2005)

Dodge Charger | 1974 | 5.2l V8 | 318 cu.in. | 150hp | 0-60: 10.3 secs | ¼ mile: 17.9 secs

5 KILLERS (2010)

Pontiac Firebird Trans Am | 1979 | 6.6l V8 | 400 cu.in. | 220hp | 0-60: 6.9 secs | ¼ mile: 15.8 secs

6 THELMA & LOUISE (1991)

Ford Thunderbird | 1967 | 6.4l V8 | 390 cu.in. | 315hp | 0-60: 9.1 secs | ¼ mile: 16.6 secs

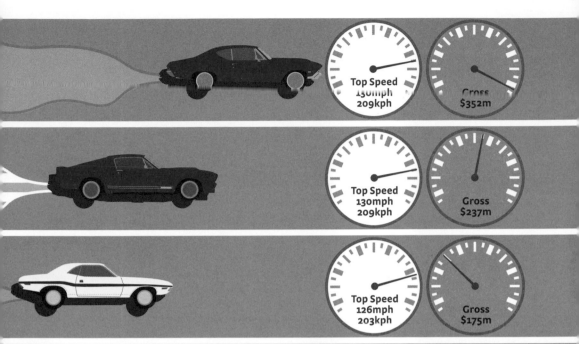

Top Speed
130mph
209kph

Gross
$352m

Top Speed
130mph
209kph

Gross
$237m

Top Speed
126mph
203kph

Gross
$175m

THE **GETAWAY**

American cars have starred in American movies since they were first made (see 1903's The Runaway Match), and not just for chase scenes or running away. These cars have all been at the centre of the plot in hit films, and surprisingly it isn't the fastest or most powerful car that's starred in the most successful movie.

Top Speed
111mph
179kph

Gross
$111m

Top Speed
134mph
215kph

Gross
$98m

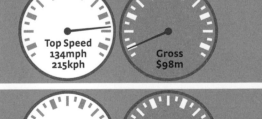

Top Speed
124mph
200kph

Gross
$78m

HOW TO MAKE A **MOVIE**

It can take years for an original idea to become a smash hit movie with a sequel in the pipeline.

5%
DEVELOPMENT

3%
SCRIPT

14%
CAST

37%
MARKETING
& EXHIBITION

23%
PRODUCTION

18%
POST
PRODUCTION

There are 6 STAGES to the process
Each stage has a percentage cost:

SHOOT
of the movie,
when the **CAST** and
PRODUCTION CREW
turn the **IDEA** into
scenes that will be
edited together in

POST-PRODUCTION
by the **DIRECTOR**
and **EDITORS** who add
in sound, special effects
and soundtrack while
the **PRODUCERS** begin
to engage

SALES
who help create
the **TRAILER** and
enter into
contracts
with

DISTRIBUTORS
for cinemas around
the world to show
the **MOVIE** after it
has had its

HOLLYWOOD

START
Your **IDEA** for a movie is good enough to attract a

PRODUCER
who starts the process of

PACKAGING
your (and now his/her) idea to a

WRITER
who begins work on the

SCRIPT DEVELOPMENT
while the **PRODUCER** creates a budget, financial plan and schedule and identifies the **CAST, DIRECTOR, and CREW** before putting it into

PRE-PRODUCTION
and engaging **CAST, DIRECTOR** and **CREW**, creating special effects and storyboards for the

PITCH
which the **PRODUCER** takes to **PRODUCTION COMPANIES** and **FINANCIERS** to pay the **WRITER** to work on the

PREMIER
opening in all major **MARKETS** before being distributed to cinemas everywhere who have already been contacted by the movie's

MARKETING
people, who have sent out posters and ads, arranged media campaigns for the lead members of the **CAST** and sometimes the **DIRECTOR** and ensured that everyone knows about the movie before it enters its

SECOND LIFE
as a **DVD** release, **TV** movie or **GAME**, earning enough in ticket sales to go back to the original **IDEA** and make a

SEQUEL
or possibly even a **FRANCHISE**, which means you never get to

THE END

45

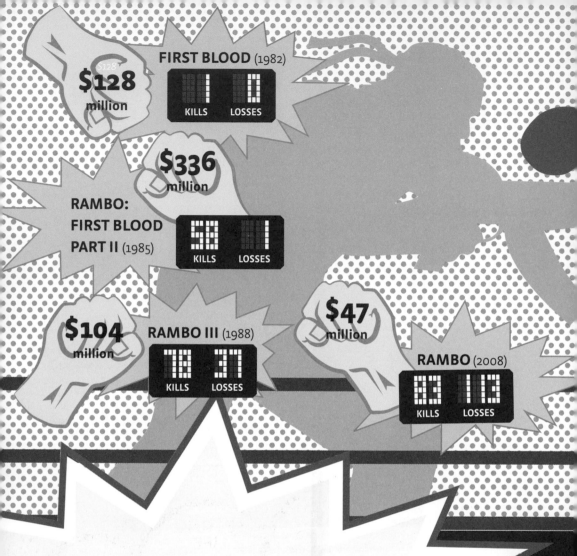

FIRST BLOOD (1982)

$128 million

KILLS **1**   LOSSES **0**

$336 million

RAMBO: FIRST BLOOD PART II (1985)

KILLS **58**   LOSSES **1**

$104 million

RAMBO III (1988)

KILLS **78**   LOSSES **37**

$47 million

RAMBO (2008)

KILLS **83**   LOSSES **113**

ROCKY **VS.** RAMBO

Sylvester Stallone's two franchise creations have been hugely successful, and his characters – the boxer Rocky Balboa and Vietnam army veteran John Rambo – have become renowned movie icons of revenge and retribution. Who has been the more successful in terms of box office and in battle, though?

ROCKY (1976)

$437 million

WINS	DRAWS	LOSSES
1	0	1

$269 million

ROCKY II (1979)

WINS	DRAWS	LOSSES
1	0	0

ROCKY III (1982)

$335 million

WINS	DRAWS	LOSSES
3	1	1

$281 million

ROCKY IV (1985)

WINS	DRAWS	LOSSES
1	0	0

ROCKY V (1990)

$77 million

WINS	DRAWS	LOSSES
2	0	0

TOTAL SCORES

ROCKY

$1.445 billion

WINS	DRAWS	LOSSES
27	1	3

RAMBO

$602.6 million

KILLS	LOSSES
220	161

$83 million

ROCKY BALBOA (2006)

WINS	DRAWS	LOSSES
1	0	1

(adjusted 2013 prices)

PUSSY GALORE

Moviemakers have long used animals as symbols and metaphors in their work to subtly give a message that might not be – but usually is – obvious to viewers.

CLICHÉ

Binx
(*Hocus Pocus*, 1993)

CUSTODY

Kitty
(*The War Of The Roses*, 1989)

COMPROMISE

Monty
(*Stuart Little*, 1999)

LASSIE

'DC'
(*That Darn Cat!* 1965 and 1997)

CONTROL

Mr Jinx
(*Meet The Parents*, 2000)

SPINSTERHOOD

B&W cat
(*The Truth About Cats & Dogs*, 1996)

MEANNESS

General Sterling Price
(*True Grit*, 1969)

REVENGE

Shadow
(*The Shadow Of The Cat*, 1961)

ZOMBIEDOM

Azezel
(*Fallen*, 1998)

PERMISSIVENESS

Cosmic Creepers
(*Bedknobs And Broomsticks*, 1971)

MEGALOMANIA

Blofeld's Persian white
Various Bond movies (1963-74)

FEMININITY

Miss Kitty
(*Batman Returns*, 1992)

CHILD'S PLAY

What do successful child movie stars want to do when they grow up? Some stick with the picture business, but others...

KEY

Most success as an child star

Most success as an adult star

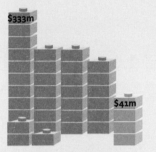

$333m

$41m

Jonathan Ke Quan
(Now a stunt coordinator)

Indiana Jones And The Temple Of Doom (1984)

California Man (1992)

$100m

Danny Lloyd
(Now a college science professor)

The Shining (1980)

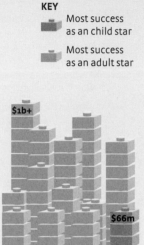

$1b+

$66m

Christian Bale
(Now an actor)

Empire Of The Sun (1987)

The Dark Knight Rises (2012)

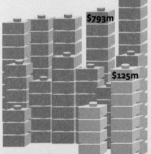

$793m

$125m

Drew Barrymore
(Now an actor)

ET (1982)

Charlie's Angels (2000)

$301m

Jasen Fisher
(Now a poker player)

Hook (1991)

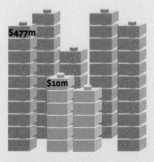

$477m

$10m

Macaulay Culkin
(Now an actor)

Home Alone (1990)

Saved (2004)

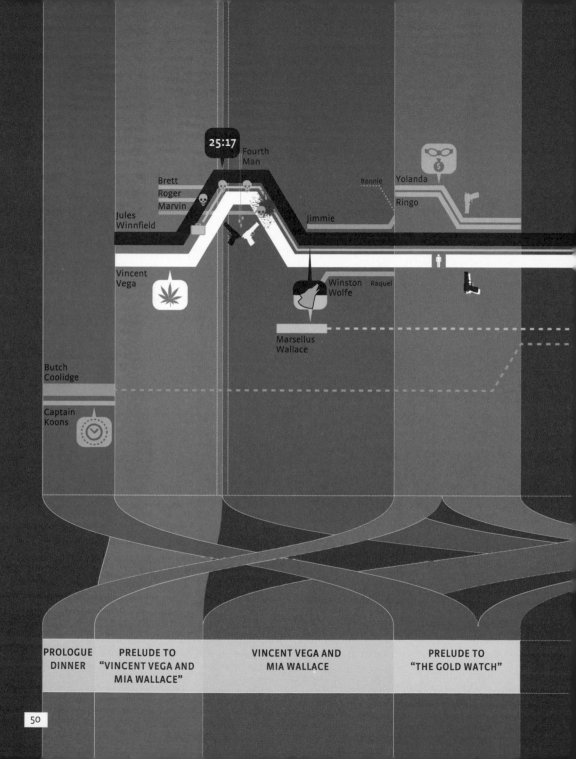

25:17

Fourth Man

Yolanda

Bonnie

Brett
Roger
Marvin

Ringo

Jules
Winnfield

Jimmie

Vincent
Vega

Winston
Wolfe

Raquel

Marsellus
Wallace

Butch
Coolidge

Captain
Koons

PROLOGUE
DINNER

PRELUDE TO
"VINCENT VEGA AND
MIA WALLACE"

VINCENT VEGA AND
MIA WALLACE

PRELUDE TO
"THE GOLD WATCH"

HOW TO READ **PULP FICTION**

Follow this timeline for Pulp Fiction. It has been arranged to show the movie chapters in chronological sequence. All character interactions and events are shown in continuity, with the original movie sequence running as a reference along the bottom.

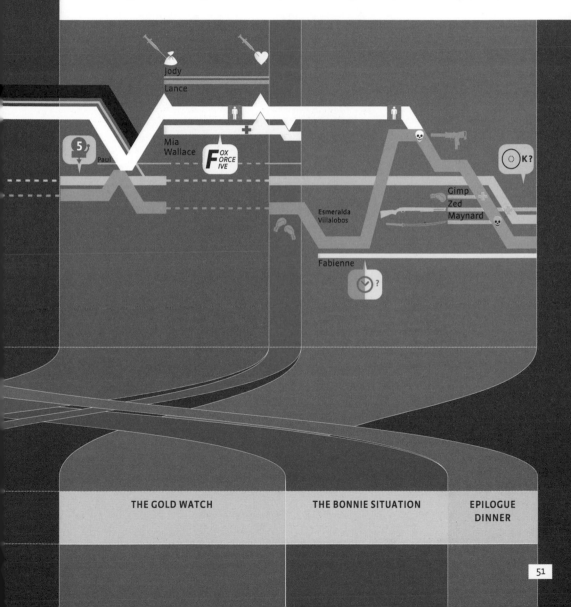

Jody
Lance
Mia Wallace
Paul

FOX ORCE IVE

Esmeralda Villalobos

Gimp
Zed
Maynard

K?

Fabienne
?

THE GOLD WATCH   **THE BONNIE SITUATION**   **EPILOGUE DINNER**

AND THE WINNER
SHOULD HAVE BEEN...

A dozen movies that perhaps should have won the Best Film Oscar, but didn't – and the movies that did win that year.

Won the Oscar

Lost the Oscar

% rottentomatoes.com rating

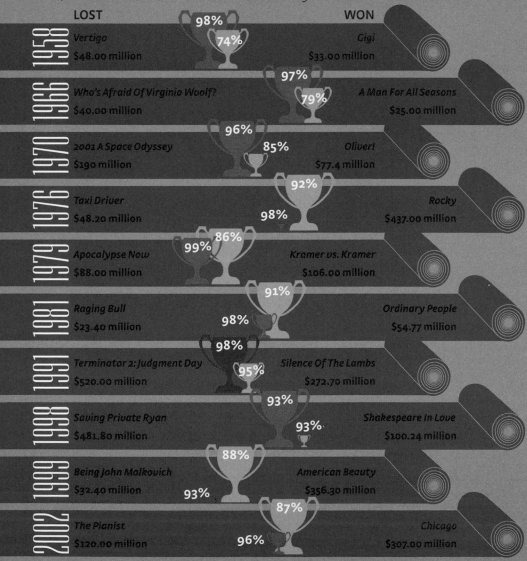

LOST   98%   **WON**

1958
Vertigo — 74% — *Gigi*
$48.00 million $33.00 million

1966
97%
Who's Afraid Of Virginia Woolf?   79%   *A Man For All Seasons*
$40.00 million $25.00 million

1970
96%
2001 A Space Odyssey   85%   *Oliver!*
$190 million $77.4 million

1976
92%
Taxi Driver   98%   *Rocky*
$48.20 million $437.00 million

1979
99%   86%
Apocalypse Now   *Kramer vs. Kramer*
$88.00 million $106.00 million

1981
91%
Raging Bull   98%   *Ordinary People*
$23.40 million $54.77 million

1991
98%
Terminator 2: Judgment Day   95%   *Silence Of The Lambs*
$520.00 million $272.70 million

1998
93%
Saving Private Ryan   93%   *Shakespeare In Love*
$481.80 million $100.24 million

1999
88%
Being John Malkovich   *American Beauty*
$32.40 million   93% $356.30 million

2002
87%
The Pianist   *Chicago*
$120.00 million   96% $307.00 million

Information courtesy of IMDb (http://www.imdb.com). Used with permission.

100% **LOSERS**

Ten movies with a 100% score on rottentomatoes.com that didn't win an Oscar that year, and those with a lesser score that did.

Winner of the Academy Award

100% Loser

100% LOSER				WINNER	
Citizen Kane (dir. Orson Welles)	100%	89%		How Green Was My Valley (dir. John Ford)	1941
The Third Man (dir. Carol Reed)	100%	96%		All The King's Men (dir. Robert Rossen)	1949
The Searchers (dir. John Ford)	100%	73%		Around The World In 80 Days (dir. Michael Anderson)	1956
North By Northwest (dir. Alfred Hitchcock)	100%	89%		Ben Hur (dir. William Wyler)	1959
Dr Strangelove (dir. Stanley Kubrick)	100%	95%		My Fair Lady (dir. George Cukor, Scott Heming)	1964
Repulsion (dir. Roman Polanski)	100%	84%		The Sound Of Music (dir. Robert Wise)	1965
Jaws (dir. Steven Spielberg)	100%	96%		One Flew Over The Cuckoo's Nest (dir. Milos Forman)	1975
Fanny Och Alexander (dir. Ingmar Bergman)	100%	89%		Gandhi (dir. Richard Attenborough)	1982
Toy Story (dir. John Lasseter)	100%	81%		Braveheart (dir. Mel Gibson)	1995
Waste Land (dir. Lucy Walker)	100%	94%		The King's Speech (dir. Tom Hooper)	2010

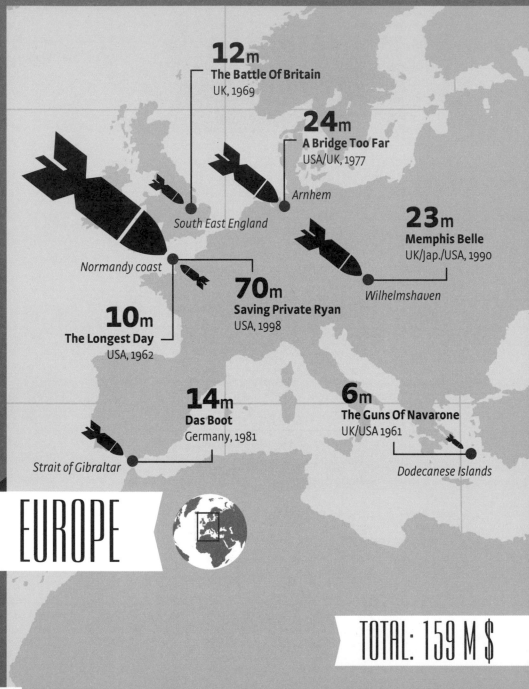

12m
The Battle Of Britain
UK, 1969

24m
A Bridge Too Far
USA/UK, 1977

Arnhem

South East England

23m
Memphis Belle
UK/Jap./USA, 1990

Normandy coast

Wilhelmshaven

70m
Saving Private Ryan
USA, 1998

10m
The Longest Day
USA, 1962

14m
Das Boot
Germany, 1981

6m
The Guns Of Navarone
UK/USA 1961

Strait of Gibraltar

Dodecanese Islands

EUROPE

TOTAL: 159 M $

THE COST OF **WWII** (THE MOVIE)

The battles of WWII became the subject of numerous big-budget movies in the decades following the conflict. Oddly, just as it was in the real conflict, Americans spent more money in Asia than they did in Europe. The dollar figures listed are the budgets for each movie (according to www.IMDb.com).

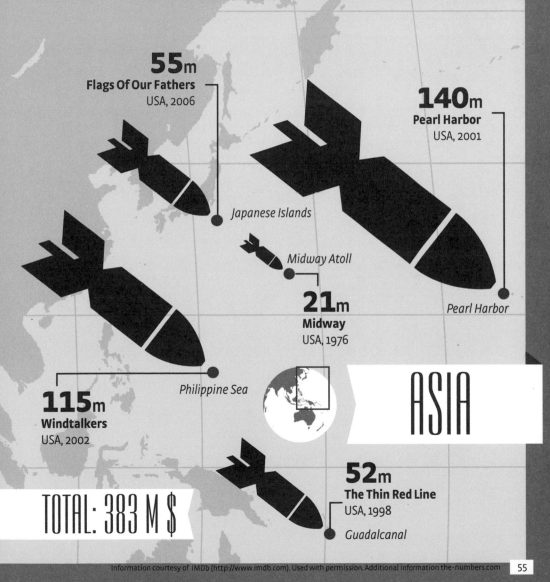

55m
Flags Of Our Fathers
USA, 2006

Japanese Islands

140m
Pearl Harbor
USA, 2001

Midway Atoll

21m
Midway
USA, 1976

Pearl Harbor

Philippine Sea

115m
Windtalkers
USA, 2002

ASIA

TOTAL: 383 M $

52m
The Thin Red Line
USA, 1998

Guadalcanal

ALFRED HITCHCOCK
PRESENTS...

The master director liked working with actors for as long as he and they could stand it. Character actors Clare Greet (1872–1939) and Leo G. Carroll (1892–1972) never appeared together in a Hitchcock movie, although both can be seen in some of his best work from 1929 (Murder!; Greet) to 1959 (North By Northwest; Carroll).

12
FREQUENTLY CAST
ACTORS AND
ACTRESSES

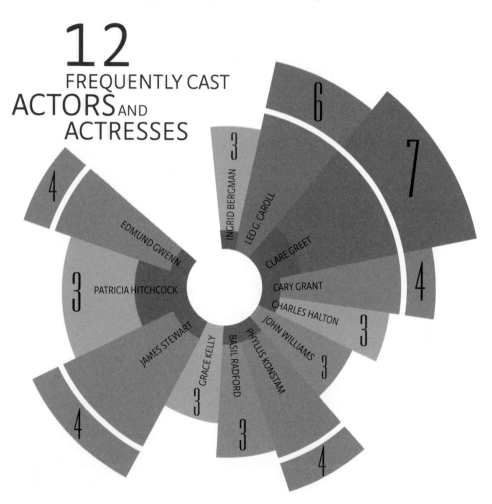

PREDICTING THE **FUTURE**

It's the business of sci-fi movies to predict what the future might look like, and how we might live. The devices shown here were predicted by films made decades prior to their invention.

A Year of film's release
B Year film's prediction realized

Jet Packs In 1939, *Buck Rogers In The 25th Century* (USA) – set in 2440 – uses Jet Packs; the first working jet pack would be successfully demonstrated in use in 1961.

Small Headphones In 1966, *Fahrenheit 451*, set in the 24th century, predicts small earphones; these would first be introduced in 1995.

Total Body Scanners In 1990, *Total Recall* (USA) uses full body scans as security screens; total body scanners would first be introduced at Schiphol Airport, Amsterdam, in 2007.

Cell Phones In 1984, *Star Trek III The Search For Spock* (USA) features characters using personal, hand-held communication devices, as had the original 1966 TV series set in 2200+; in both instances, they resemble the mobile phones of the late 1990s.

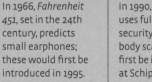

Videophone calls In 1927, *Metropolis* (Ger.), set in 2026, predicts the use of videophones; the first public videophone – Picturephone – would be demonstrated in 1964.

In 1989, *Back To The Future II* (USA), set in 2015, has a videophone conversation on a flat screen TV in the McFly household; Skype would be introduced in 2003.

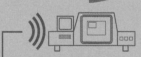

Voice-activated Computer In 1976, *The Hitchhiker's Guide To The Galaxy* (UK) has a voice-controlled computer (as does *Blade Runner*, USA, 1982); the first voice activation system would be introduced in the 2000s.

Commercial Space Travel In 1929, *Frau Im Mond* (Ger.) predicts travel to the moon in a multi-stage rocket using liquid fuel and the reverse countdown; in 1969, man would make the first moon landing using a 3-stage rocket and liquid fuel.

In 1950, *Destination Moon* (USA) predicts private investment in moon and space missions; in 2011, Virgin would announce privately financed space travel.

DONE TO **DEATH** AT HOME

In every home there are a multitude of everyday items that can be – and have been – used by moviemakers as deadly weapons.

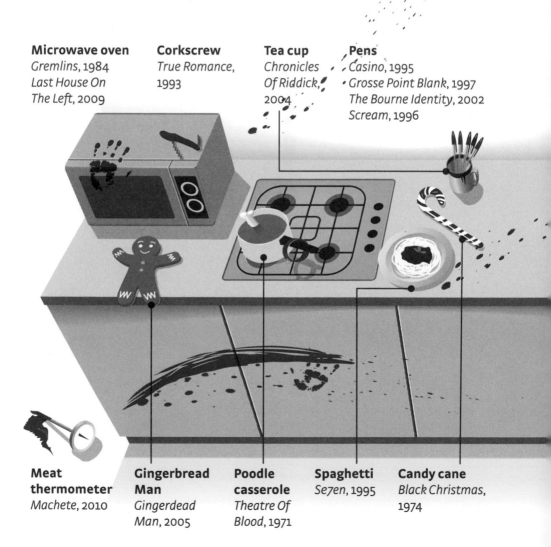

Microwave oven
Gremlins, 1984
Last House On The Left, 2009

Corkscrew
True Romance, 1993

Tea cup
Chronicles Of Riddick, 2004

Pens
Casino, 1995
Grosse Point Blank, 1997
The Bourne Identity, 2002
Scream, 1996

Meat thermometer
Machete, 2010

Gingerbread Man
Gingerdead Man, 2005

Poodle casserole
Theatre Of Blood, 1971

Spaghetti
Se7en, 1995

Candy cane
Black Christmas, 1974

Pencil
The Evil Dead, 1981
The Dark Knight, 2008

Televison set
*Henry, Portrait Of
A Serial Killer*, 1986
Grosse Pointe Blank, 1997

Refrigerator
The Refrigerator, 1991

Chopsticks
Fireworks,
1997

Chili Pepper
*Jackie Chan's Project A:
Part 2*, 1987

Blender
Gremlins,
1984

Corn
Witness, 1985
Sleepwalkers, 1992
Scary Movie 2, 2001

Carrot
Shoot 'Em Up, 2007

Peanut
Daredevil,
2003

**T-bone
from steak**
*Law Abiding
Citizen*, 2009

Leg of lamb
Serial Mom,
1994

THE JUDD APATOW
FORMULA

In 2007 Entertainment Weekly named director, writer and producer Judd Apatow the smartest person in Hollywood after the huge success of The 40-Year-Old-Virgin and Knocked Up. Has he found a formula that works?

● Male lead: single, nerdy, uptight and insecure

■ Male lead: single, stoner and insecure

▲ Female lead: smart, in control, mother

⬡ Buddy male second lead: conformist, drinker with a wife/partner

★ Male antagonist: obnoxious

									GROSS
Celtic Pride (1996)	■				+	★	=		**$9m**
Heavyweights (1995)	●				+	★	=		**$18m**
Walk Hard: The Dewey Cox Story (2007)	■						=		**$18m**
Funny People (2009)	●	+ ▲	+ ⬡		+	★	=		**$52m**
This Is 40 (2012)	■	+ ▲	+ ⬡		+	★	=		**$65m**
The 40 Year-Old-Virgin (2005)	●	+ ▲	+ ⬡				=		**$109m**
Fun With Dick And Jane (2005)	●	+ ▲			+	★	=		**$110m**
Knocked Up (2007)	■	+ ▲	+ ⬡				=		**$149m**

Giving more weight to the ingredients that appear in the highest grossing films, the composition of the ultimate Judd Apatow movie might be...

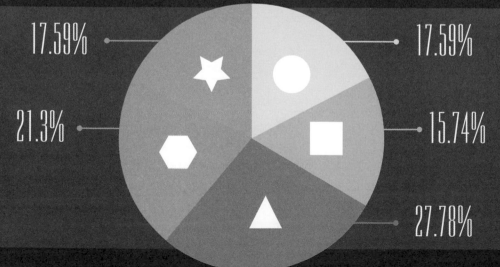

17.59%
17.59%
21.3%
15.74%
27.78%

 Information courtesy of Box Office Mojo. Used with permission.

THE **DEVIL'S DRESS SENSE**

What Hollywood's most successful portrayals of Satan have worn.

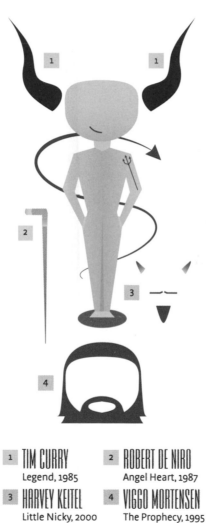

PETER STORMARE
Constantine
2005

JENNIFER LOVE HEWITT
Shortcut To Happiness
2003

AL PACINO
The Devil's Advocate
1997

1 **TIM CURRY**
Legend, 1985

2 **ROBERT DE NIRO**
Angel Heart, 1987

3 **HARVEY KEITEL**
Little Nicky, 2000

4 **VIGGO MORTENSEN**
The Prophecy, 1995

JACK NICHOLSON
The Witches Of Eastwick
1987

ROSALINDA CELENTANO
The Devil's Advocate
1997

ELIZABETH HURLEY
Bedazzled
2000

A WORLD OF **VILLAINS**

Only a fifth of the actors playing baddies in the eight top-grossing Hollywood action thriller movie franchises are American born. Half are British. That's some special relationship...

AC Michael Wincott *Gary Soneji* **B** Joseph Wiseman *Dr Julius No* **BO** Nicky Naudé *Castel* **X** Tyler Mane *Sabretooth*

AC Matthew Fox *Picasso* **B** Christopher Walken *Max Zorin* Yaphet Kotto *Dr Kananga* Robert Davi *Franz Sanchez* Joe Don Baker *Brad Whitaker* Richard Kiel *Jaws* **BO** Louis Ozawa Changchien *LARX-3* **DH** William Sadler *Colonel Stuart* Timothy Olyphant *Thomas Gabriel* Maggie Q *Mai Linh* **MI** Jon Voight *Jim Phelps* Philip Seymour Hoffman *Owen Davian*

B Robert Carlyle *Renard* Viktor Zokas *Blofeld* Anthony Dawson *Blofeld* **IJ** Michael Sheard *Adolf Hitler* **MI** Dougray Scott *Sean Ambrose* **X** Brian Cox *Colonel Stryker*

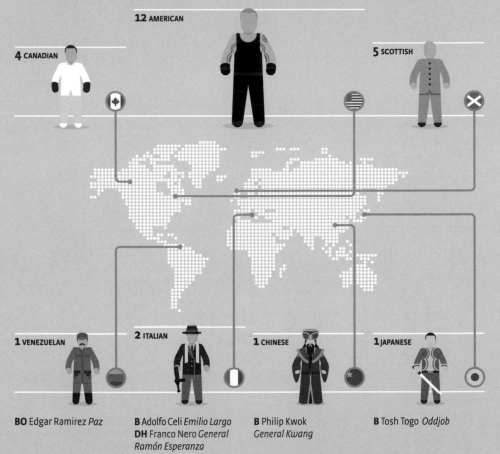

12 AMERICAN

4 CANADIAN

5 SCOTTISH

1 VENEZUELAN

2 ITALIAN

1 CHINESE

1 JAPANESE

BO Edgar Ramirez *Paz*

B Adolfo Celi *Emilio Largo* **DH** Franco Nero *General Ramón Esperanza*

B Philip Kwok *General Kwang*

B Tosh Togo *Oddjob*

AC	*Alex Cross*	**BO**	*Bourne*	**IJ**	*Indiana Jones*	**JR**	*Jack Reacher*
B	*Bond*	**DH**	*Die Hard*	**MI**	*Mission Impossible*	**X**	*X-Men*

AC Cary Elwes *Nick Ruskin* **B** Sean Bean *Janus* Steven Berkoff *General Orlov* Charles Gray *Blofeld* Julian Glover *Aristotle Kristatos* John Hollis *wheelchair villain* Christopher Lee *Scaramanga* Rosamund Pike *Miranda Frost* Donald Pleasence *Blofeld* Robert Rietty *wheelchair villain* Toby Stephens *Gustav Graves* **BO** Russell Levy *Mannheim* Clive Owen *The Professor* **DH** Alan Rickman *Hans Gruber* Jeremy Irons *Simon Gruber* **IJ** Michael Byrne *Colonel Ernst Vogel* Paul Freeman *René Belloq* Julian Glover *Walter Donovan* Ronald Lacey *Major Arnold Toht* Pat Roach *mine overseer* Ray Winstone *George Mac Michale* **MI** Eddie Marsan *Brownway* **X** Vinnie Jones *Juggernaut* Ian McKellen *Magneto*

B Jeroen Krabbé *General Georgi Koskov* **X** Famke Janssen *Phoenix* Rebecca Romijn-Stamos *Mystique*

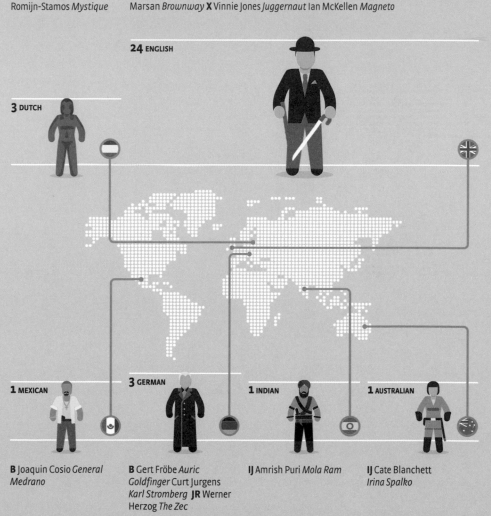

24 ENGLISH

3 DUTCH

1 MEXICAN

3 GERMAN

1 INDIAN

1 AUSTRALIAN

B Joaquin Cosio *General Medrano*

B Gert Fröbe *Auric Goldfinger* Curt Jurgens *Karl Stromberg* **JR** Werner Herzog *The Zec*

IJ Amrish Puri *Mola Ram*

IJ Cate Blanchett *Irina Spalko*

Information courtesy of IMDb (http://www.imdb.com). Used with permission.

TRUE BOX OFFICE **GOLD**

In 1930 some 65% of the American population went to the cinema weekly. By 1964 that number had fallen to 10% (when there were 1.04bn tickets sold). It has remained pretty much steady ever since, which may explain why the top 30 grossing movies in America, even when adjusted for inflation*, are oldies.

Gone With The Wind 1939	$1.63B
Star Wars 1977	$1.43B
The Sound Of Music 1964	$1.15B
ET: The Extra-Terrestrial 1982	$1.14B
Titanic 1997	$1.09B
The Ten Commandments 1956	$1.05B
Jaws 1977	$1.03B
Doctor Zhivago 1965	$999M
The Exorcist 1973	$890M
Snow White And The Seven Dwarfs 1937	$877M
101 Dalmatians 1961	$804M
The Empire Strikes Back 1980	$790M
Ben-Hur 1959	$789M
Avatar 2009	$783M
Return Of The Jedi 1983	$757M

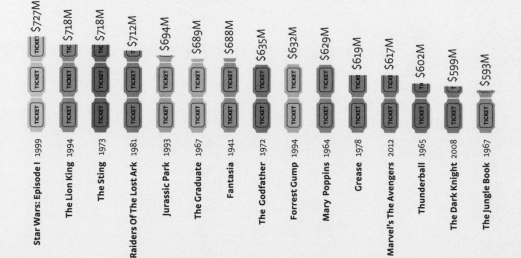

Movie	Year	Gross
Star Wars: Episode I	1999	$727M
The Lion King	1994	$718M
The Sting	1973	$718M
Raiders Of The Lost Ark	1981	$712M
Jurassic Park	1993	$694M
The Graduate	1967	$689M
Fantasia	1941	$688M
The Godfather	1972	$635M
Forrest Gump	1994	$632M
Mary Poppins	1964	$629M
Grease	1978	$619M
Marvel's The Avengers	2012	$617M
Thunderball	1965	$602M
The Dark Knight	2008	$599M
The Jungle Book	1967	$593M

*(adjusted for inflation to 2013 prices at $8.20 per ticket)

NORTH AMERICA

Québec (2)

Ontario (4)

Massachusetts (5)

New England (2)

British Columbia (6)

Ohio (2)

WI

Washington (2)

MI

Missouri (4)

IL

NJ

CT

New York (9)

UT

CO

DE

AZ

Kentucky (5)

Pennsylvania (10)

Maryland (2)

New Mexico (3)

WV

NC

VA

SC

TN

Georgia (2)

Louisiana (4)

Saint Sebastian (4)

Texas (3)

Florida (5)

Haiti (2)

California (32)

Cayman (1)

Bahamas (1)

Brazil (2)

SOUTH AMERICA

New Zealand (2)

Chile (1)

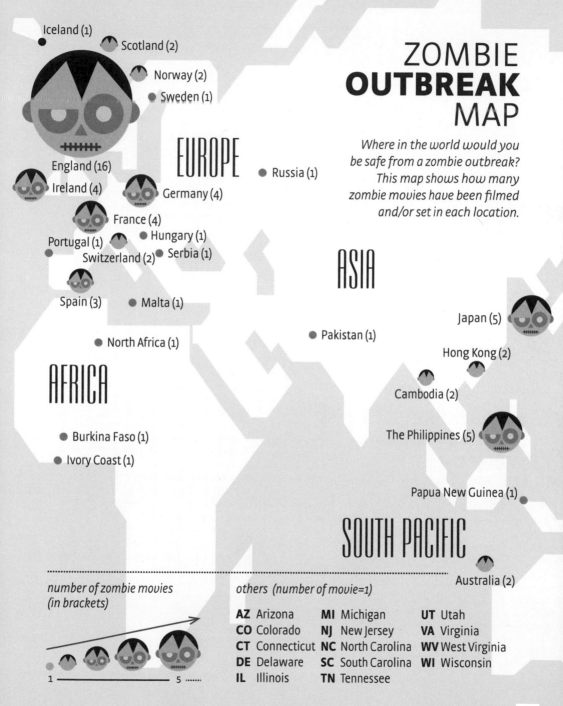

ZOMBIE **OUTBREAK** MAP

Where in the world would you be safe from a zombie outbreak? This map shows how many zombie movies have been filmed and/or set in each location.

Iceland (1)

Scotland (2)

Norway (2)

Sweden (1)

England (16)

EUROPE

Russia (1)

Ireland (4)

Germany (4)

France (4)

Portugal (1)

Hungary (1)

Switzerland (2)

Serbia (1)

Spain (3)

Malta (1)

ASIA

Pakistan (1)

Japan (5)

Hong Kong (2)

North Africa (1)

Cambodia (2)

AFRICA

The Philippines (5)

Burkina Faso (1)

Ivory Coast (1)

Papua New Guinea (1)

SOUTH PACIFIC

Australia (2)

number of zombie movies (in brackets)

1 ————— 5 ·······

others *(number of movie=1)*

AZ Arizona	**MI** Michigan	**UT** Utah
CO Colorado	**NJ** New Jersey	**VA** Virginia
CT Connecticut	**NC** North Carolina	**WV** West Virginia
DE Delaware	**SC** South Carolina	**WI** Wisconsin
IL Illinois	**TN** Tennessee	

NET **PROFITS**

Even the most successful Hollywood films rarely seem to go into profit. As these sample costs for a major Hollywood movie (based on actual costs of a franchise hit) demonstrate, that's because there are ever-increasing costs incurred by studios as they exploit the movie in different formats and markets.

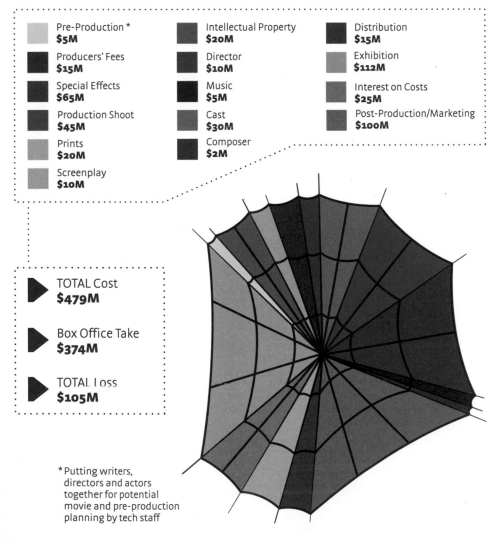

Pre-Production *
$5M

Producers' Fees
$15M

Special Effects
$65M

Production Shoot
$45M

Prints
$20M

Screenplay
$10M

Intellectual Property
$20M

Director
$10M

Music
$5M

Cast
$30M

Composer
$2M

Distribution
$15M

Exhibition
$112M

Interest on Costs
$25M

Post-Production/Marketing
$100M

TOTAL Cost
$479M

Box Office Take
$374M

TOTAL Loss
$105M

*Putting writers, directors and actors together for potential movie and pre-production planning by tech staff

ANIMAL **REVENGE**

*Don't go in the water! Amphibious reptiles and flesh-eating fish
are by far the most deadly animals in the movie kingdom.*

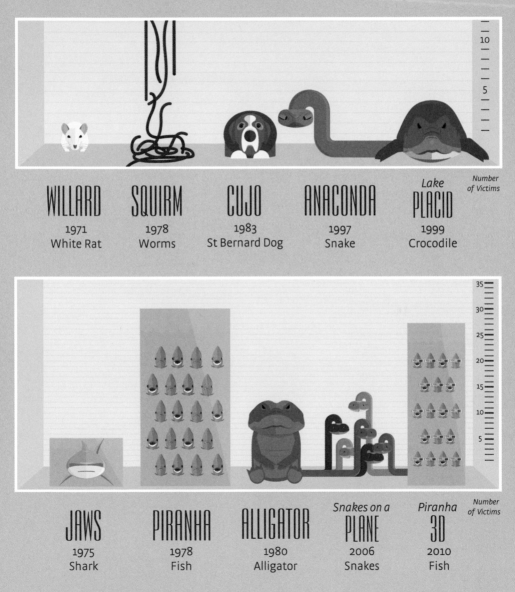

Number of Victims

WILLARD	SQUIRM	CUJO	ANACONDA	Lake PLACID
1971	1978	1983	1997	1999
White Rat	Worms	St Bernard Dog	Snake	Crocodile

Number of Victims

JAWS	PIRANHA	ALLIGATOR	Snakes on a PLANE	Piranha 3D
1975	1978	1980	2006	2010
Shark	Fish	Alligator	Snakes	Fish

IT'S IN THE
GAME

Many multi-million – or even billion – selling video game franchises have been turned into large screen movie franchises, but it hasn't always been a successful transition. As demonstrated by this chart of bestselling video game franchises contrasted with their movie versions.

KEY

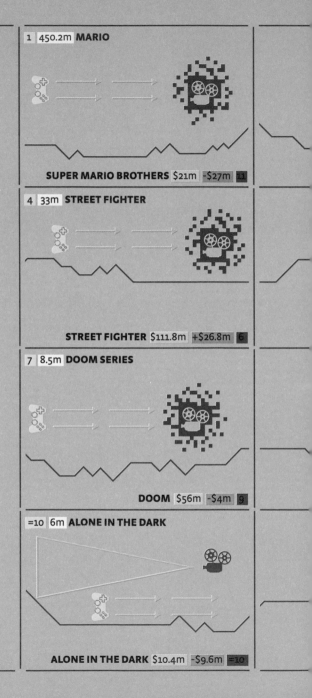

Video game rank

Video game units sold

Film rank

Film profit / loss

Film gross

Video game wins

Video game loses

Film wins

Film loses

---

1 450.2m **MARIO**

SUPER MARIO BROTHERS $21m -$27m **11**

4 33m **STREET FIGHTER**

STREET FIGHTER $111.8m +$26.8m **6**

7 8.5m **DOOM SERIES**

DOOM $56m -$4m **9**

=10 6m **ALONE IN THE DARK**

ALONE IN THE DARK $10.4m -$9.6m **=10**

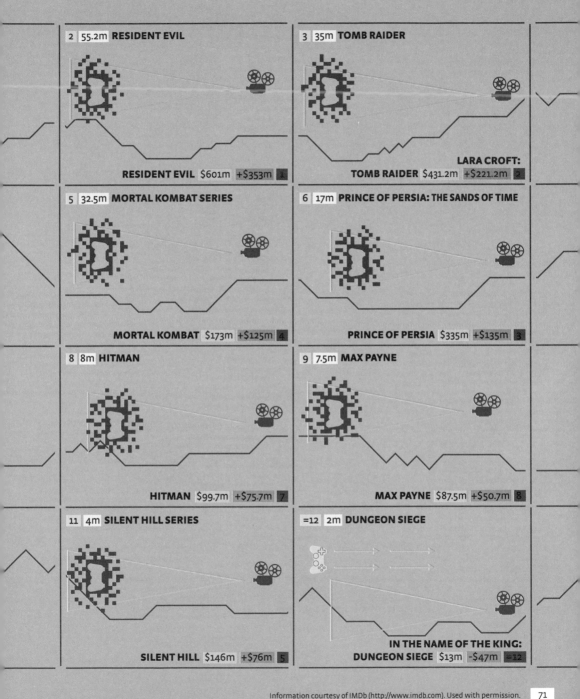

2 | 55.2m | **RESIDENT EVIL**

RESIDENT EVIL $601m +$353m **1**

3 | 35m | **TOMB RAIDER**

LARA CROFT: TOMB RAIDER $431.2m +$221.2m **2**

5 | 32.5m | **MORTAL KOMBAT SERIES**

MORTAL KOMBAT $173m +$125m **4**

6 | 17m | **PRINCE OF PERSIA: THE SANDS OF TIME**

PRINCE OF PERSIA $335m +$135m **3**

8 | 8m | **HITMAN**

HITMAN $99.7m +$75.7m **7**

9 | 7.5m | **MAX PAYNE**

MAX PAYNE $87.5m +$50.7m **8**

11 | 4m | **SILENT HILL SERIES**

SILENT HILL $146m +$76m **5**

=12 | 2m | **DUNGEON SIEGE**

IN THE NAME OF THE KING: DUNGEON SIEGE $13m -$47m **=12**

HOLLYWOOD'S
HIGHEST PAID

THE OLYMPIA

ON RODEO DRIVE

THE TWILIGHT SAGA: BREAKING DAWN PART 1

MARK WAHLBERG

TED

CONTRABAND

THE PERFECT STORM

WILL SMITH

THE TWILIGHT SAGA: BREAKING DAWN PART 2

THE TWILIGHT SAGA: NEW MOON

TAYLOR LAUTNER

HARRY POTTER AND THE GOBLET OF FIRE

BEL AMI

WATER FOR ELEPHANTS

ROBERT PATTINSON

THE IVY

RESTAURANT

TOP GUN

ROCK OF AGES

MISSION IMPOSSIBLE

TOM CRUISE

TITANIC

J EDGAR

HAVANA ROOM

In 2011–12 the 11 actors shown in this graphic were the highest paid in their profession (according to Forbes). Here are their estimated earnings and releases for that year, plus their key hit movies.

DJANGO UNCHAINED

LEONARDO DICAPRIO

THE WATERBOY

JACK AND JILL

THAT'S MY BOY

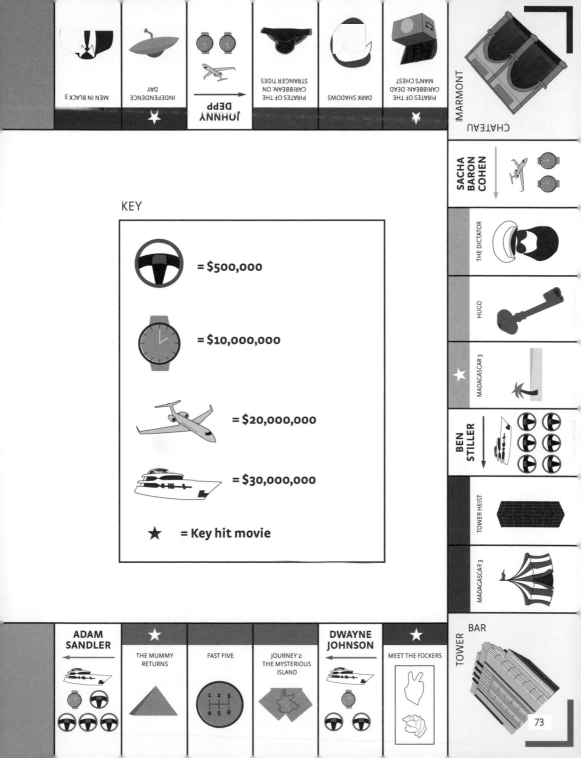

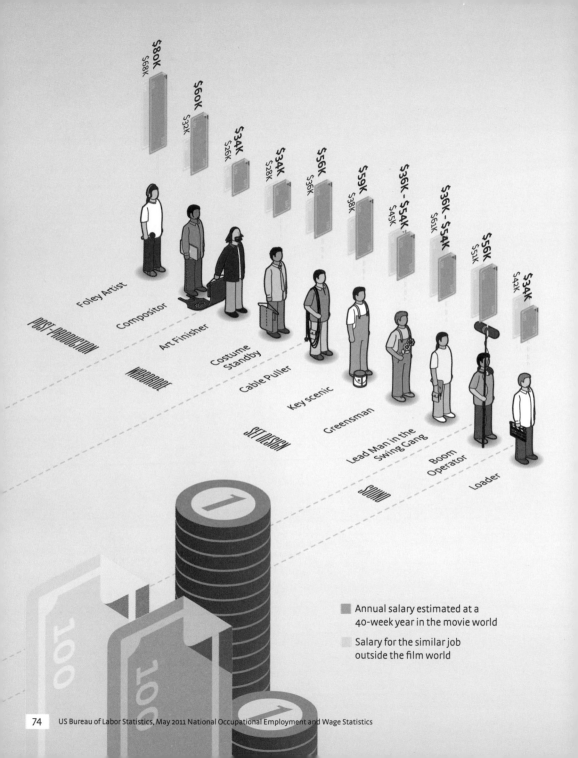

$80K
$68K
$60K
$32K
$34K
$26K
$34K
$28K
$56K
$36K
$59K
$38K
$36K - $54K
$45K
$36K - $54K
$61K
$56K
$55K
$34K
$42K

POST-PRODUCTION
Foley Artist
Compositor
Art Finisher

WARDROBE
Costume Standby
Cable Puller

SET DESIGN
Key scenic
Greensman
Lead Man in the Swing Gang

SOUND
Boom Operator
Loader

Annual salary estimated at a 40-week year in the movie world

Salary for the similar job outside the film world

BEST BOYS, DOLLY GRIPS AND A **WRANGLER**

Here are the salaries of all those odd-sounding roles that run in the end credits of movies.

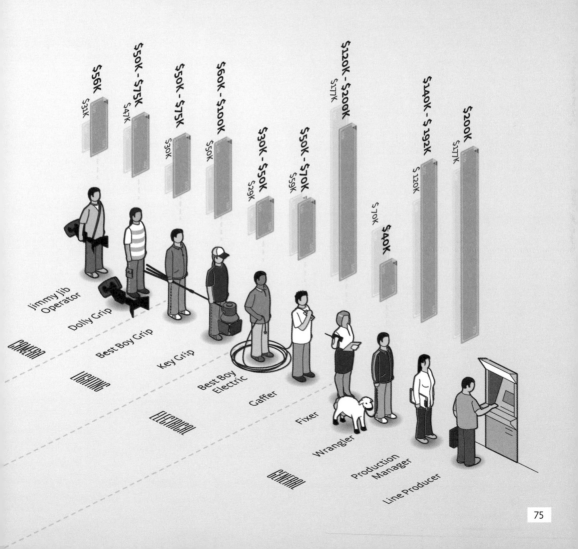

$56K
$31K
Jimmy Jib Operator

$50K - $75K
$47K
Dolly Grip

$50K - $75K
$30K
Best Boy Grip

$60K - $100K
$50K
Key Grip

$30K - $50K
$29K
Best Boy Electric

$50K - $70K
$59K
Gaffer

$120K - $200K
$177K
Fixer

$70K
$40K
Wrangler

$140K - $192K
$120K
Production Manager

$200K
$177K
Line Producer

CAMERA

LIGHTING

ELECTRICAL

GENERAL

IN THE SHADE WITH
TOM CRUISE

Gauging Tom Cruise's wearing of sunglasses and the box office success of his movies, it seems that the more he appears in sunglasses, the more his audience like him...

Average Rank

Use of Sunglasses

Light, <10

None, 0

RANK OF BOX OFFICE SUCCESS

TOM CRUISE MOVIES

Far And Away (1992)

Interview With The Vampire (1994)

Eyes Wide Shut (1999)

The Last Samurai (2003)

The Outsiders (1983)

The Color Of Money (1986)

Cocktail (1988)

Born On The Fourth Of July (1989)

A Few Good Men (1992)

The Firm (1993)

Minority Report (2002)

Days Of Thunder (1990)

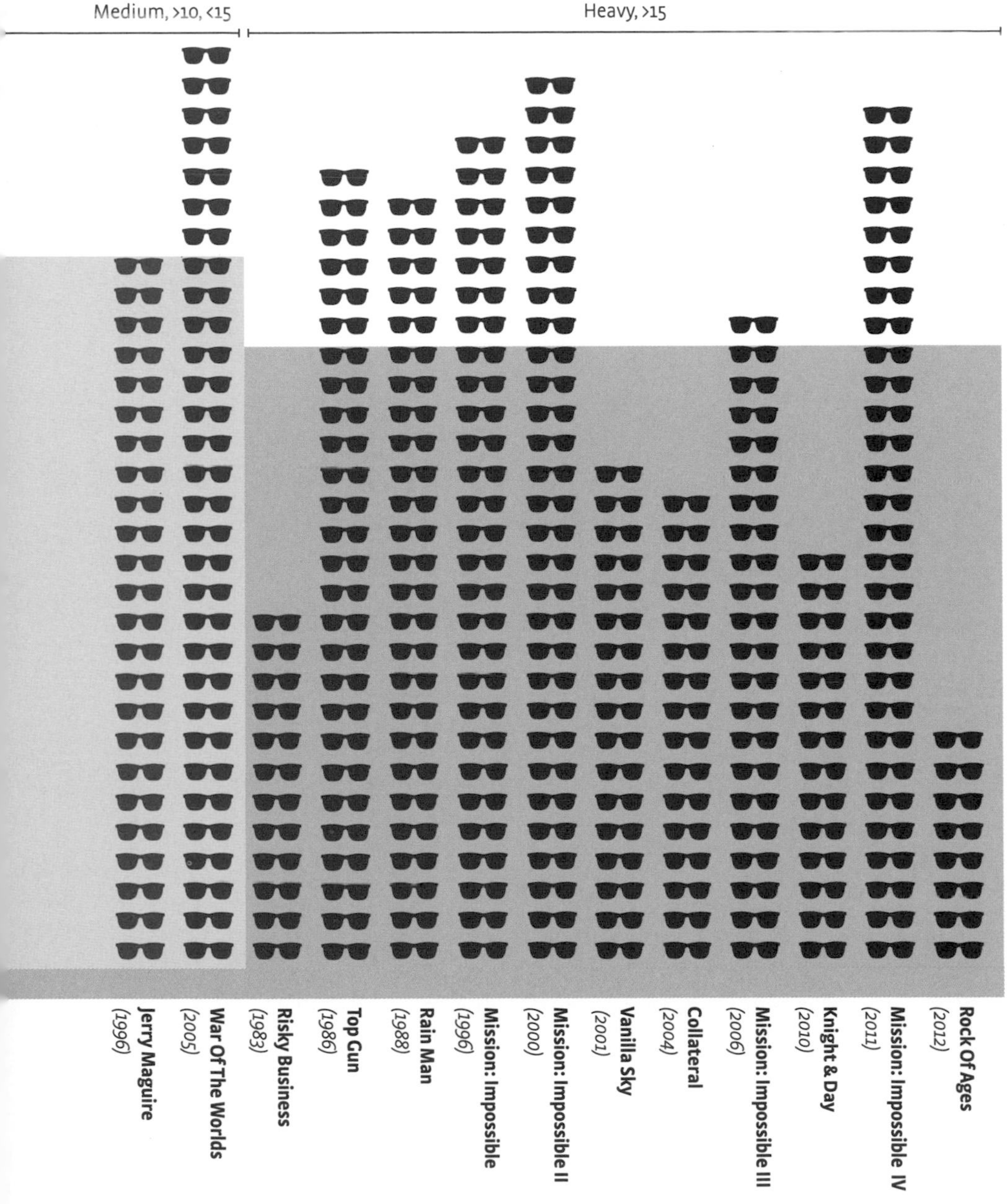
Medium, >10, <15
Heavy, >15
Jerry Maguire (1996)
War Of The Worlds (2005)
Risky Business (1983)
Top Gun (1986)
Rain Man (1988)
Mission: Impossible (1996)
Mission: Impossible II (2000)
Vanilla Sky (2001)
Collateral (2004)
Mission: Impossible III (2006)
Knight & Day (2010)
Mission: Impossible IV (2011)
Rock Of Ages (2012)

THE **FINAL** SCORE

Original movie musical soundtracks are an integral part of the business, yet often little attention is paid to the men (there are few female composers in the field) who create them. These are the top 10 composers' career box office successes up to 2013.

1 Hans Zimmer, German

2 John Williams, American

3 James Newton Howard, American

4 Alan Silvestri, American

5 James Horner, American

6 Danny Elfman, American

7 John Powell, English

8 John Debney, American

9 Howard Shore, Canadian

10 Jerry Goldsmith, American

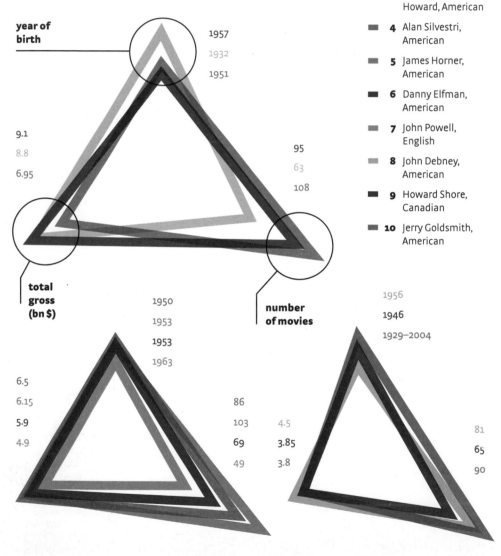

year of birth

1957
1932
1951

total gross (bn $)

9.1
8.8
6.95

number of movies

95
63
108

1950
1953
1953
1963

6.5
6.15
5.9
4.9

86
103
69
49

4.5
3.85
3.8

1956
1946
1929–2004

81
65
90

NAME THAT MOVIE **1990S**

Use these graphics to identify the titles of ten memorable films from the 1990s. The first letter of each film title is included to help you identify it.

NOT LOST IN TRANSLATION

Not all successful movies in the world are made in English. All of the films here are the biggest cinema hits in their homeland. Some became (subtitled) international hits.

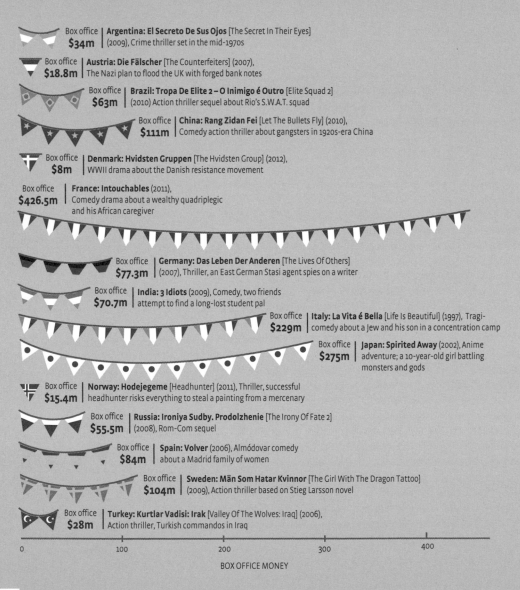

Box office **$34m** | **Argentina: El Secreto De Sus Ojos** [The Secret In Their Eyes] (2009), Crime thriller set in the mid-1970s

Box office **$18.8m** | **Austria: Die Fälscher** [The Counterfeiters] (2007), The Nazi plan to flood the UK with forged bank notes

Box office **$63m** | **Brazil: Tropa De Elite 2 – O Inimigo é Outro** [Elite Squad 2] (2010) Action thriller sequel about Rio's S.W.A.T. squad

Box office **$111m** | **China: Rang Zidan Fei** [Let The Bullets Fly] (2010), Comedy action thriller about gangsters in 1920s-era China

Box office **$8m** | **Denmark: Hvidsten Gruppen** [The Hvidsten Group] (2012), WWII drama about the Danish resistance movement

Box office **$426.5m** | **France: Intouchables** (2011), Comedy drama about a wealthy quadriplegic and his African caregiver

Box office **$77.3m** | **Germany: Das Leben Der Anderen** [The Lives Of Others] (2007), Thriller, an East German Stasi agent spies on a writer

Box office **$70.7m** | **India: 3 Idiots** (2009), Comedy, two friends attempt to find a long-lost student pal

Box office **$229m** | **Italy: La Vita é Bella** [Life Is Beautiful] (1997), Tragi-comedy about a Jew and his son in a concentration camp

Box office **$275m** | **Japan: Spirited Away** (2002), Anime adventure; a 10-year-old girl battling monsters and gods

Box office **$15.4m** | **Norway: Hodejegeme** [Headhunter] (2011), Thriller, successful headhunter risks everything to steal a painting from a mercenary

Box office **$55.5m** | **Russia: Ironiya Sudby. Prodolzhenie** [The Irony Of Fate 2] (2008), Rom-Com sequel

Box office **$84m** | **Spain: Volver** (2006), Almódovar comedy about a Madrid family of women

Box office **$104m** | **Sweden: Män Som Hatar Kvinnor** [The Girl With The Dragon Tattoo] (2009), Action thriller based on Stieg Larsson novel

Box office **$28m** | **Turkey: Kurtlar Vadisi: Irak** [Valley Of The Wolves: Iraq] (2006), Action thriller, Turkish commandos in Iraq

0   100   200   300   400

BOX OFFICE MONEY

Information courtesy of IMDb (http://www.imdb.com). Used with permission.

BEATLES **VS.** STONES ON FILM

The Beatles are the most successful pop band in history, but excluding their own movies their recordings have made surprisingly few appearances in movies. Their great rivals the Rolling Stones, however, can be heard on many more original soundtracks.

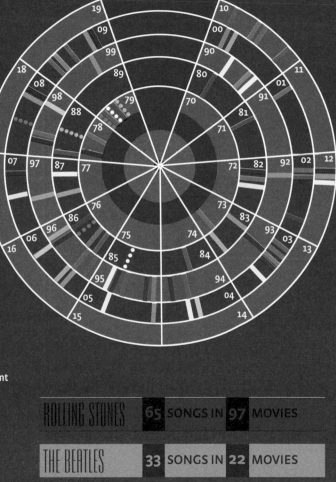

Songs used in more than one movie

BEATLES
- Twist And Shout
- I Want To Hold Your Hand
- I Saw Her Standing There

ROLLING STONES
- Sympathy For The Devil
- Gimme Shelter
- Satisfaction
- Jumpin' Jack Flash
- Wild Horses
- Beast Of Burden
- Can't You Hear Me Knocking
- Street Fighting Man
- Shattered
- Miss You
- Let's Spend The Night Together
- You Can't Always Get What You Want
- Play With Fire
- Let It Loose
- 19th Nervous Breakdown
- Paint It Black
- Time Is On My Side
- Waiting On A Friend

ROLLING STONES **65** SONGS IN **97** MOVIES

THE BEATLES **33** SONGS IN **22** MOVIES

POPCORN OR FRESH
FRUIT AND **VEGETABLES**?

US-based research into how many calories are contained in medium and large popcorn and soda combos sold at three major cinema chains found that on average customers were consuming between 1200 and 1600 calories while watching a movie. Imagine if the cinemas sold only fruit and vegetables instead!

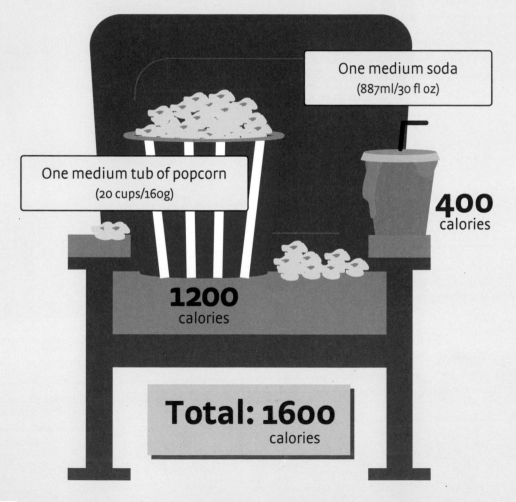

One medium soda
(887ml/30 fl oz)

One medium tub of popcorn
(20 cups/160g)

400
calories

1200
calories

Total: 1600
calories

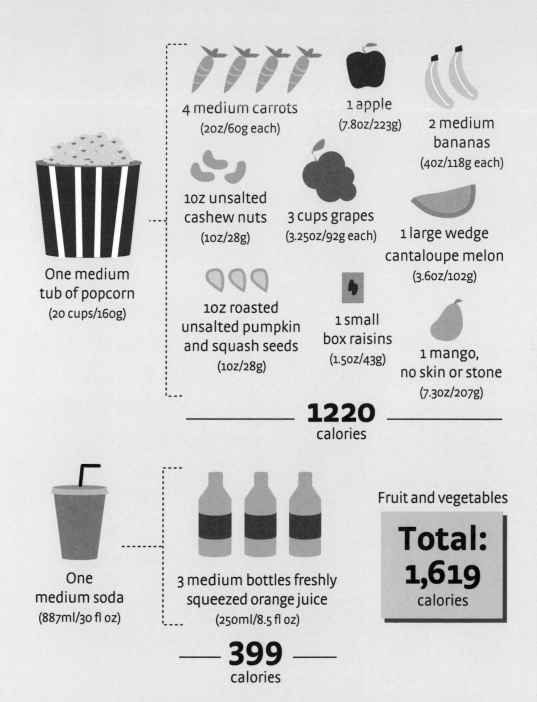

One medium tub of popcorn (20 cups/160g)

4 medium carrots (2oz/60g each)

1 apple (7.8oz/223g)

2 medium bananas (4oz/118g each)

1oz unsalted cashew nuts (1oz/28g)

3 cups grapes (3.25oz/92g each)

1 large wedge cantaloupe melon (3.6oz/102g)

1oz roasted unsalted pumpkin and squash seeds (1oz/28g)

1 small box raisins (1.5oz/43g)

1 mango, no skin or stone (7.3oz/207g)

1220 calories

One medium soda (887ml/30 fl oz)

3 medium bottles freshly squeezed orange juice (250ml/8.5 fl oz)

399 calories

Fruit and vegetables

Total: 1,619 calories

2009 report by Center for Science in the Public Interest, published in Nutrition Action Newsletter
http://www.webmd.com/food-recipes/news/20091119/movie-theater-popcorn-a-calorie-bomb; caloriecount.about.com

TAXI OR TRANSPORTER?

French writer-director-producer Luc Besson really knows how to work a good thing. After huge European success with a series of films titled Taxi (I–IV), he created the Transporter series of movies for the American and European market. The two franchises have a lot in common...

Budget (millions $)

Hero's car

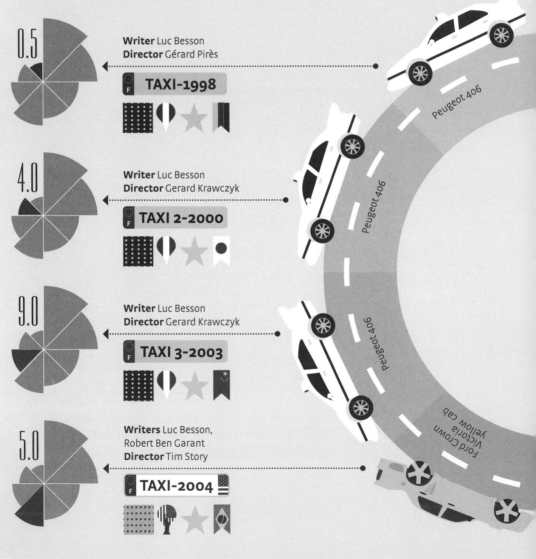

0.5

Writer Luc Besson
Director Gérard Pirès

TAXI-1998

4.0

Writer Luc Besson
Director Gerard Krawczyk

TAXI 2-2000

9.0

Writer Luc Besson
Director Gerard Krawczyk

TAXI 3-2003

5.0

Writers Luc Besson,
Robert Ben Garant
Director Tim Story

TAXI-2004

Peugeot 406

Peugeot 406

Peugeot 406

Ford Crown
Victoria
Yellow cab

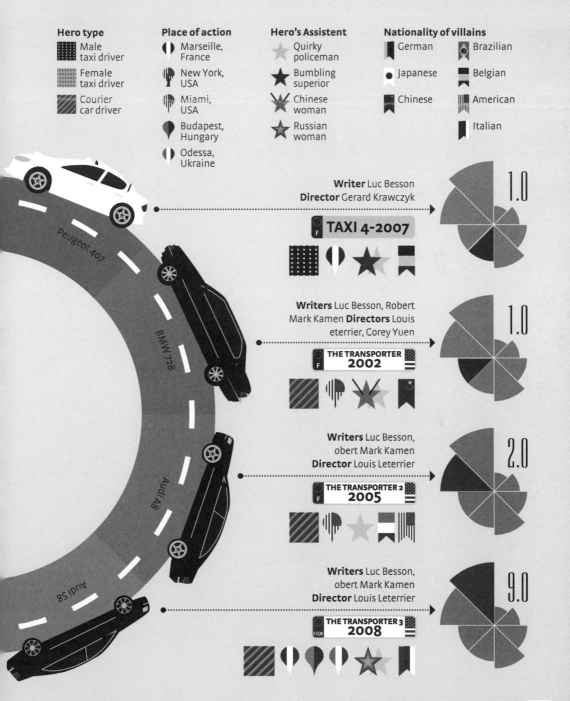

Hero type
- Male taxi driver
- Female taxi driver
- Courier car driver

Place of action
- Marseille, France
- New York, USA
- Miami, USA
- Budapest, Hungary
- Odessa, Ukraine

Hero's Assistent
- Quirky policeman
- Bumbling superior
- Chinese woman
- Russian woman

Nationality of villains
- German
- Japanese
- Chinese
- Brazilian
- Belgian
- American
- Italian

Peugeot 407

BMW 728

Audi A8

Audi S8

Writer Luc Besson
Director Gerard Krawczyk

TAXI 4-2007

1.0

Writers Luc Besson, Robert Mark Kamen **Directors** Louis eterrier, Corey Yuen

THE TRANSPORTER 2002

1.0

Writers Luc Besson, obert Mark Kamen
Director Louis Leterrier

THE TRANSPORTER 2 2005

2.0

Writers Luc Besson, obert Mark Kamen
Director Louis Leterrier

THE TRANSPORTER 3 2008

9.0

ATTACK CLINT!

Clint Eastwood has starred in 67 movies, and in most of them he suffers some kind of physical assault, which often appears critical. However, he's only died three times in movies (The Beguiled, Honkytonk Man, Gran Turino), the rest of the time he recovers from his injuries. Here's how they're inflicted.

136 head bludgeoned with blunt instrument

12 eyes gouged

51 nose punched

132 mouth punched

145 knuckles bruised

hanging 2

shoulder wounded (bullet) 9

arm wounded (bullet) 12

heart broken 3

152 arm wounded (blade)

ribs beaten and/or stomped 66

160 stomach punched or kneed

15 stomach poisoned

0 soul destroyed

10 groin kicked

ass kicked 83

7 leg wounded (bullet)

leg wounded (bullet) 7

2 leg wounded (knife/arrow)

leg wounded (knife/arrow) 2

foot broken 1

HEAVEN'S **GATE**

What is the right age for an actor to be when playing a deity in a film? The average age is calculated using data from every person to have portrayed God, Jesus, Zeus or Elvis in a major movie.

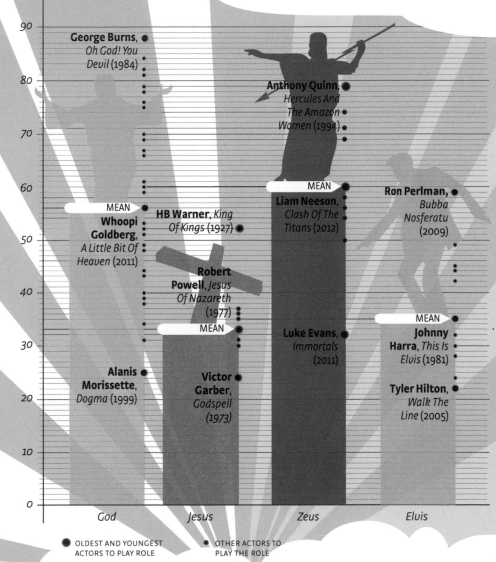

Age

90 —
80 —
70 —
60 —
50 —
40 —
30 —
20 —
10 —
0 —

George Burns, *Oh God! You Devil (1984)*

Anthony Quinn, *Hercules And The Amazon Women (1994)*

MEAN

Ron Perlman, *Bubba Nosferatu (2009)*

MEAN

Whoopi Goldberg, *A Little Bit Of Heaven (2011)*

HB Warner, *King Of Kings (1927)*

Liam Neeson, *Clash Of The Titans (2012)*

Robert Powell, *Jesus Of Nazareth (1977)*

MEAN

Luke Evans, *Immortals (2011)*

MEAN

Johnny Harra, *This Is Elvis (1981)*

Alanis Morissette, *Dogma (1999)*

Victor Garber, *Godspell (1973)*

Tyler Hilton, *Walk The Line (2005)*

God   Jesus   Zeus   Elvis

● OLDEST AND YOUNGEST ACTORS TO PLAY ROLE

• OTHER ACTORS TO PLAY THE ROLE

UNEQUAL
DISTRIBUTION

Between 1995 and 2012 six movie distribution companies made up more than 75% of the US market by $ gross. Between them they distributed more than 2500 movies and earned more than $144bn.

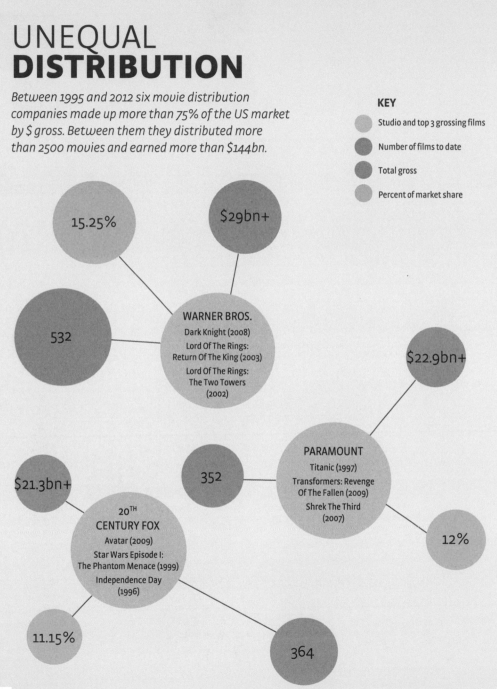

KEY

- Studio and top 3 grossing films
- Number of films to date
- Total gross
- Percent of market share

15.25%

$29bn+

532

WARNER BROS.
Dark Knight (2008)
Lord Of The Rings:
Return Of The King (2003)
Lord Of The Rings:
The Two Towers
(2002)

$22.9bn+

PARAMOUNT
Titanic (1997)
Transformers: Revenge
Of The Fallen (2009)
Shrek The Third
(2007)

352

$21.3bn+

**20TH
CENTURY FOX**
Avatar (2009)
Star Wars Episode I:
The Phantom Menace (1999)
Independence Day
(1996)

12%

11.15%

364

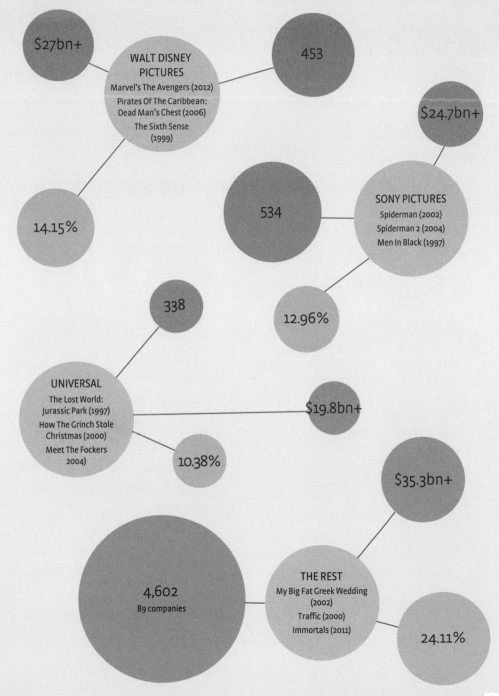

$27bn+

WALT DISNEY
PICTURES

Marvel's The Avengers (2012)

Pirates Of The Caribbean:
Dead Man's Chest (2006)

The Sixth Sense
(1999)

453

$24.7bn+

14.15%

534

SONY PICTURES

Spiderman (2002)
Spiderman 2 (2004)
Men In Black (1997)

12.96%

338

UNIVERSAL

The Lost World:
Jurassic Park (1997)

How The Grinch Stole
Christmas (2000)

Meet The Fockers
2004)

$19.8bn+

10.38%

$35.3bn+

4,602
89 companies

THE REST

My Big Fat Greek Wedding
(2002)

Traffic (2000)

Immortals (2011)

24.11%

ROAD **TRIP**

What way did they go? From Easy Rider *to* Smokey And The Bandit, *and from* Thelma & Louise *to* On The Road – *four cinematic journeys across America.*

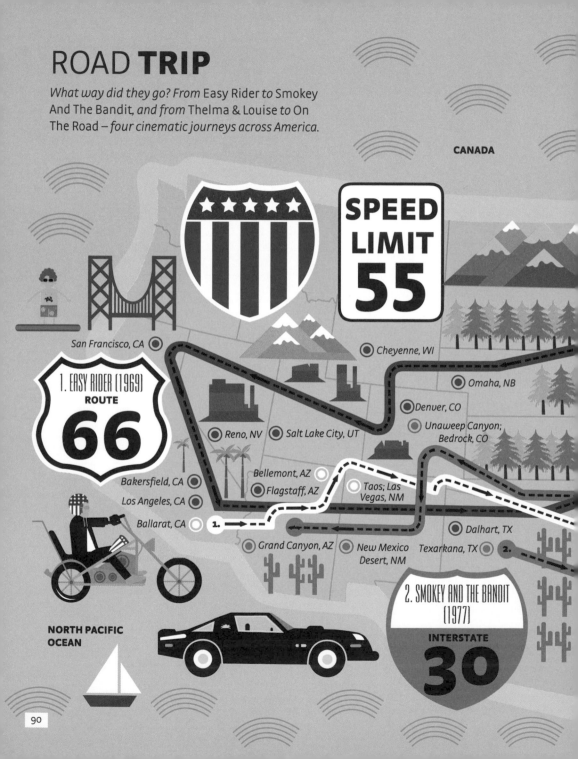

CANADA

SPEED LIMIT **55**

San Francisco, CA ⊙

1. EASY RIDER (1969)
ROUTE
66

⊙ Cheyenne, WI

⊙ Omaha, NB

⊙ Denver, CO

⊙ Reno, NV   ⊙ Salt Lake City, UT

⊙ Unaweep Canyon; Bedrock, CO

Bakersfield, CA ⊙
Los Angeles, CA ⊙
Ballarat, CA ⊙   **1.** →

Bellemont, AZ ⊙
Flagstaff, AZ ⊙

Taos; Las Vegas, NM ⊙

⊙ Dalhart, TX

⊙ Grand Canyon, AZ   New Mexico Desert, NM

Texarkana, TX ⊙   **2.**

NORTH PACIFIC OCEAN

2. SMOKEY AND THE BANDIT (1977)
INTERSTATE
30

90

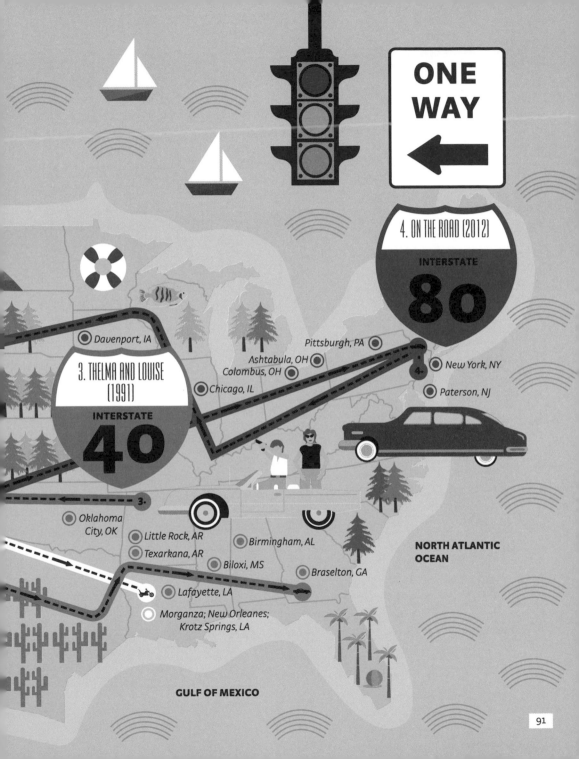

ONE WAY

4. ON THE ROAD (2012)

INTERSTATE

80

3. THELMA AND LOUISE (1991)

INTERSTATE

40

Davenport, IA

Pittsburgh, PA

Ashtabula, OH
Colombus, OH

New York, NY

Chicago, IL

Paterson, NJ

3.

Oklahoma
City, OK

Little Rock, AR

Birmingham, AL

Texarkana, AR

NORTH ATLANTIC
OCEAN

Biloxi, MS

Braselton, GA

Lafayette, LA

Morganza; New Orleanes;
Krotz Springs, LA

GULF OF MEXICO

I-SPY

The success of the James Bond movies (based on 12 novels and two short story collections) in the early 1960s launched a host of imitators on both the small and big screen. The Bond-alikes were drawn either from a wealth of previously published books, or directly from the movie Bond.

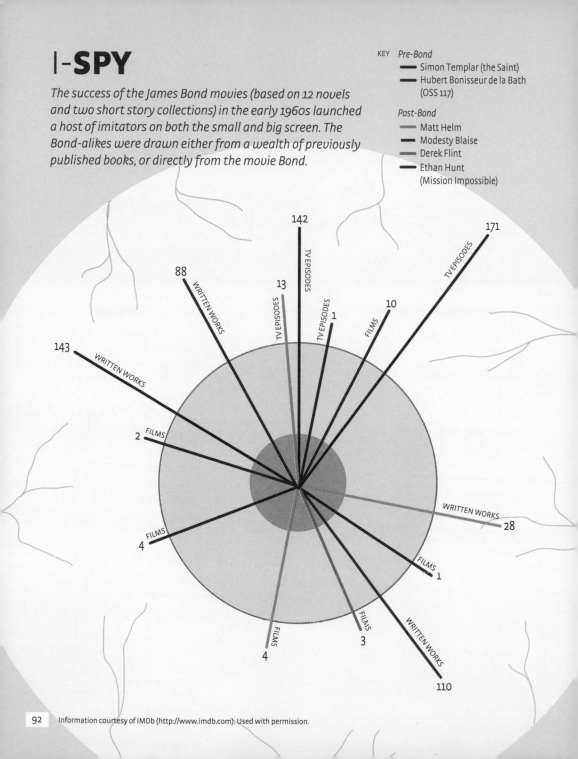

142 TV EPISODES

88 WRITTEN WORKS

13 TV EPISODES

1 TV EPISODES

10 FILMS

171 TV EPISODES

143 WRITTEN WORKS

2 FILMS

28 WRITTEN WORKS

4 FILMS

1 FILMS

4 FILMS

3 FILMS

110 WRITTEN WORKS

ALL THE **PRESIDENTS**

American presidents have not only been made in Hollywood, they've also been remade. Constantly. These are the US presidents who have appeared in a movie more than three times.

George Washington
(1789-97)

Andrew Jackson
(1829-37)
★ Charlton Heston (2)

Abraham Lincoln
(1861-65)
Frank McGlynn Jr (3)

Ulysses S Grant
(1869-77)

Theodore 'Teddy' Roosevelt
(1901-09)
★ Robin Williams

FD Roosevelt
(1933-45)
★ Jack Young (4)

Harry S Truman
(1945-53)

Dwight Eisenhower
(1953-61)

John F Kennedy
(1961-63)
★ Brett Stimely (2)

Lyndon B Johnson
(1963-69)

Richard Nixon
(1969-74)

Gerald Ford
(1974-77)

Ronald Reagan
(1981-89)
★ Jay Koch (3)

George H Bush
(1989-93)

Bill Clinton
(1993-2001)

George W Bush
(2001-09)

★ Actors who have played a president more than once

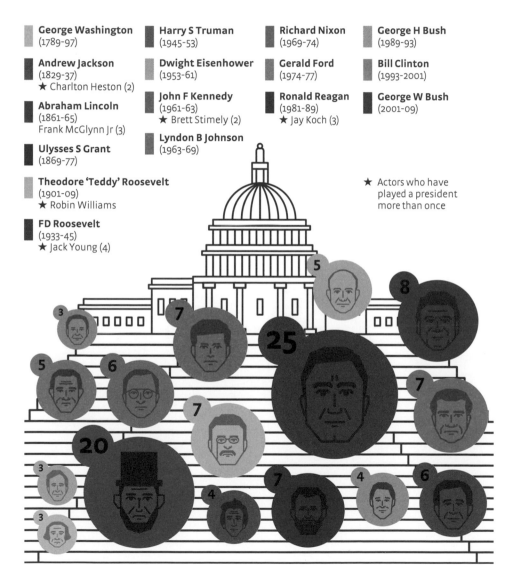

HOLLYWOOD'S **MOST** WANTED (PART 2)

The top six female actors, in terms of box office success in America, are listed in descending order. Sigourney Weaver's part in Avatar (more than $760m in sales so far) and Kathy Bates's in Titanic ($659m) gain them their rankings. Without those movies their places would be taken by Cate Blanchett (lifetime gross of $2,003m) and Anne Hathaway ($1,900m).

Cameron Diaz
* Shrek 2 (2004)

8

6

13

1

1st
$2,806m

Julia Roberts
* Ocean's Eleven (2001)

13

8

17

0

2nd
$2,504m

Emma Watson
* Harry Potter And The Deathly Hallows Part 2 (2011)

3

0

5

3

3rd
$2,473m

KEY

Films grossing **$0-$33m**

Films grossing **$67-$299m**

Films grossing **$34-$66m**

Blockbusters **($300m+)**

* = highest grossing film

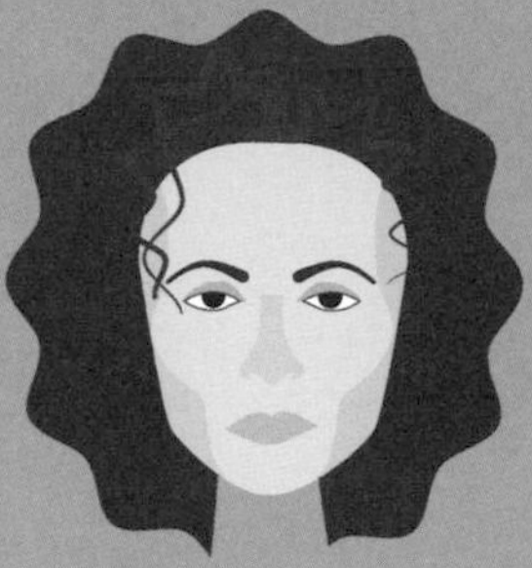

Helena Bonham Carter

* *Harry Potter And The Deathly Hallows Part 2 (2011)*

16

5

6

3

4th

$2,404m

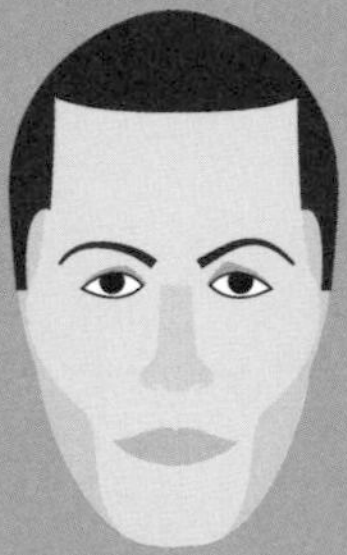

Sigourney Weaver

* *Avatar (2009)*

28

7

8

1

5th

$2,177m

Kathy Bates

* *Titanic (1997)*

27

6

8

1

6th

$2,164m

Information courtesy of Box Office Mojo. Used with permission.

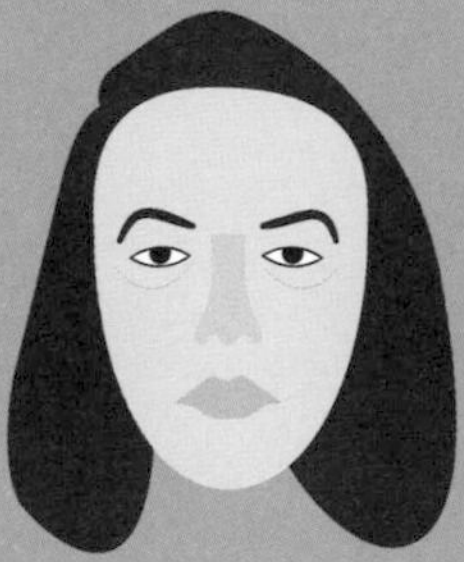

IMAGINARY **FRIENDS**

How the most famous imaginary friends in movies can be grouped. How they are eerily familiar and inter-connected.

1950 Harvey

1977 Pete's Dragon

1946 A Matter Of Life And Death

White, 6ft, drinks like a fish, named Harvey

Fire-breathing

18th-century dandy

1

1971 Mr Horatio Knibbles

1

1972 Play It Again, Sam

1996 Bogus

White, 6ft, likes kid's parties, named Mr Horatio Knibbles

Looks like Humphrey Bogart in a raincoat

20th-century magician

2001 Donnie Darko

2009 Paperman

2009 Youth In Revolt

Black, over 6ft, likes watching movies, named Frank

Captain Excellent!

20th-century alter-ego

3

2

RABBIT

FICTIONAL

FRENCH ANGEL

① Children's film   ② Lead characters are writers   ③ Young men looking for love

④ Abusive fathers   ⑤ Lead actors named Christian   ⑥ Heartbreak Hotel: soundtrack

④

1980 **The Shining**

1999 **Fight Club**

2004 **The Machinist**

2007 **Lars And The Real Girl**

⑤

Finger-talking Tony

Useful in a fight

On-demand Bianca

2010 **Charlie St Cloud**

2000 **Cast Away**

⑤

1993 **True Romance**

Baseball-playing Sam St Cloud

Great for playing soccer

⑥   ⑥

In-tune Elvis Presley

2009 **Imagine That**

2004 **Secret Window**

④

2012 **Imaginary Friend**

1

Dancing Princesses Kupida and Mopida

Good storyteller

Bitchy Brittany

②

CHILDREN

BEST BUDDY

LOVER

97

NAME THAT MOVIE **2000S**

Use these graphics to identify the titles of ten memorable films from the 2000s. The first letter of each film title is included to help you identify it.

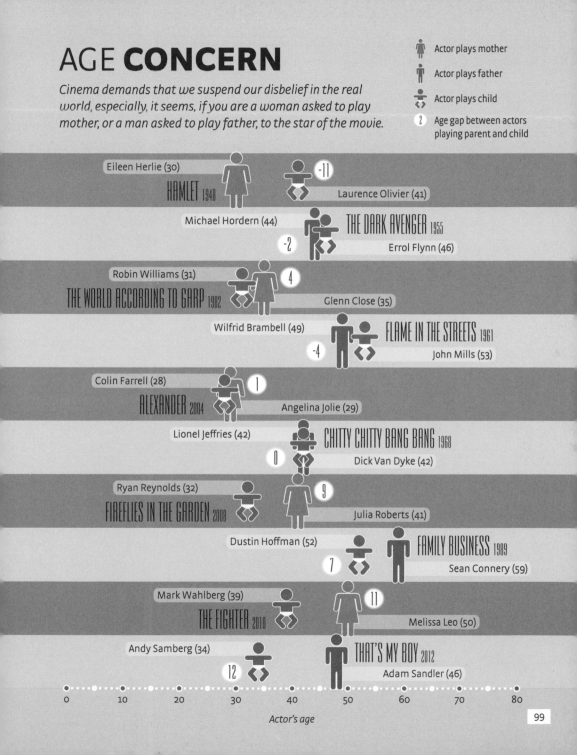

AGE **CONCERN**

Cinema demands that we suspend our disbelief in the real world, especially, it seems, if you are a woman asked to play mother, or a man asked to play father, to the star of the movie.

Actor plays mother
Actor plays father
Actor plays child
2 Age gap between actors playing parent and child

Eileen Herlie (30)
HAMLET 1948 −11
Laurence Olivier (41)

Michael Hordern (44) THE DARK AVENGER 1955
−2
Errol Flynn (46)

Robin Williams (31) 4
THE WORLD ACCORDING TO GARP 1982
Glenn Close (35)

Wilfrid Brambell (49) FLAME IN THE STREETS 1961
−4
John Mills (53)

Colin Farrell (28) 1
ALEXANDER 2004
Angelina Jolie (29)

Lionel Jeffries (42) CHITTY CHITTY BANG BANG 1968
0
Dick Van Dyke (42)

Ryan Reynolds (32)
FIREFLIES IN THE GARDEN 2008 9
Julia Roberts (41)

Dustin Hoffman (52)
FAMILY BUSINESS 1989
7
Sean Connery (59)

Mark Wahlberg (39)
THE FIGHTER 2010 11
Melissa Leo (50)

Andy Samberg (34)
THAT'S MY BOY 2012
12
Adam Sandler (46)

0 10 20 30 40 50 60 70 80

Actor's age

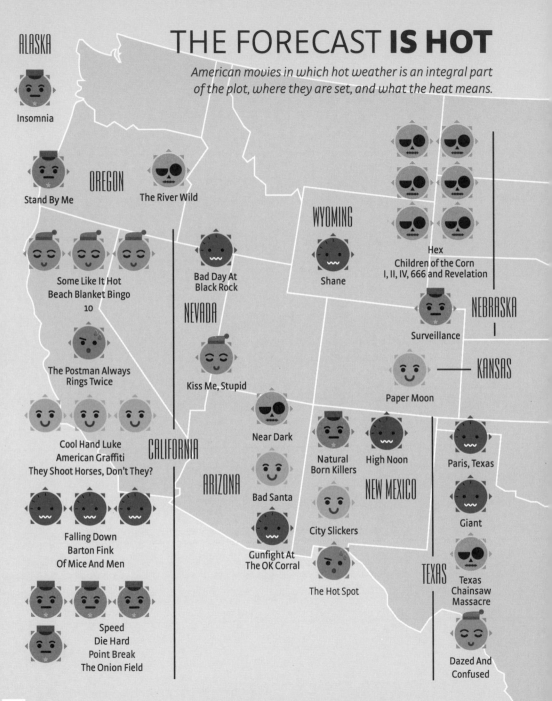

THE FORECAST **IS HOT**

American movies in which hot weather is an integral part of the plot, where they are set, and what the heat means.

ALASKA

Insomnia

OREGON

Stand By Me

The River Wild

WYOMING

Shane

Hex
Children of the Corn
I, II, IV, 666 and Revelation

NEBRASKA

Surveillance

KANSAS

Paper Moon

Some Like It Hot
Beach Blanket Bingo
10

Bad Day At
Black Rock

NEVADA

The Postman Always
Rings Twice

Kiss Me, Stupid

Cool Hand Luke
American Graffiti
They Shoot Horses, Don't They?

CALIFORNIA

Near Dark

Bad Santa

ARIZONA

Gunfight At
The OK Corral

Natural
Born Killers

High Noon

NEW MEXICO

City Slickers

The Hot Spot

Paris, Texas

Giant

TEXAS

Texas
Chainsaw
Massacre

Falling Down
Barton Fink
Of Mice And Men

Speed
Die Hard
Point Break
The Onion Field

Dazed And
Confused

Midsummer night's sex comedy

Holiday horror

On heat

Tickly heat

High pressure

Crime wave

Where the Heart Is

Bug

The Outsiders

WISCONSIN

The Great Outdoors

Grapes Of Wrath

ILLINOIS

OKLAHOMA

Rookie Of The Year
Ferris Bueller's Day Off

MISSOURI

Road House

In The Heat Of The Night

MISSISSIPPI

Drive Angry

LOUISIANA

A Streetcar Named Desire
The Big Easy

Deliverance

NORTH CAROLINA

SOUTH CAROLINA

GEORGIA

Shag

Body Heat

FLORIDA

Miami Vice
Scarface
Key Largo

What About Bob?

Summer of 42

NEW HAAMPSHIRE

NEW YORK

MASS.

Jaws

Adventureland

PENNS.

N.J.

Friday The 13th

VIRGINIA

I Know What You Did Last Summer

Cape Fear

Do The Right Thing
Dog Day Afternoon

Summer Of Sam
12 Angry Men

Dirty Dancing
9 ½ Weeks

A Midsummer Night's Sex Comedy
The Seven Year Itch

Funny Games

Die Hard With A Vengeance

FRANCIS FORD COPPOLA'S LIFE IN **PICTURES**

The American director, writer, producer and studio owner has been involved professionally in 76 movies in a 50-year career. There have been a few major successes for which he is best known (The Godfather trilogy, Apocalypse Now, etc.) but there have also been a raft of other projects.

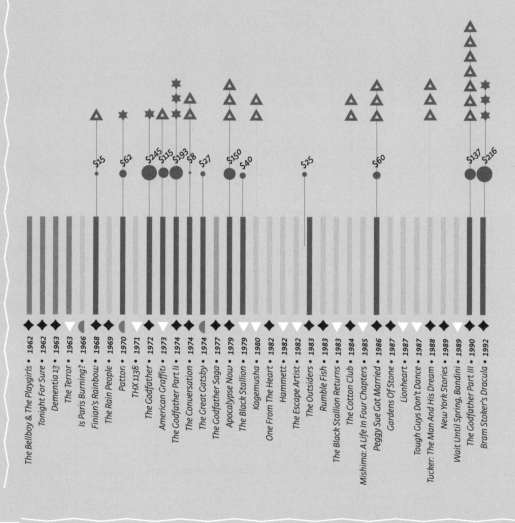

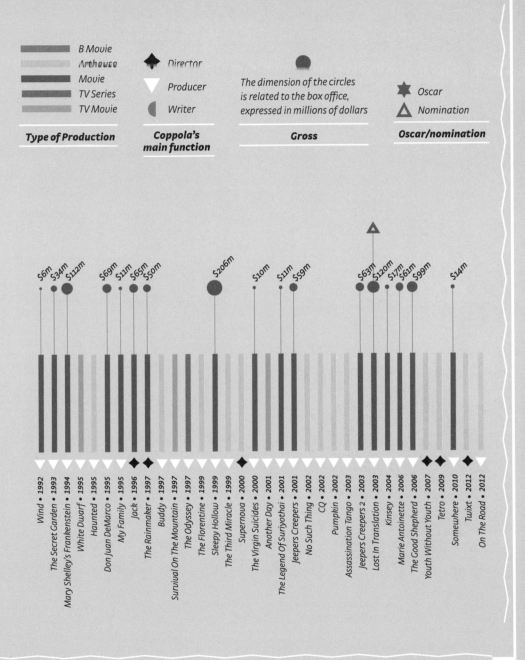

Type of Production
- B Movie
- Arthouse Movie
- Movie
- TV Series
- TV Movie

Coppola's main function
- Director
- Producer
- Writer

Gross
The dimension of the circles is related to the box office, expressed in millions of dollars

Oscar/nomination
- Oscar
- Nomination

$6m — Wind · 1992
$34m — The Secret Garden · 1993
$112m — Mary Shelley's Frankenstein · 1994
White Dwarf · 1995
Haunted · 1995
$69m — Don Juan DeMarco · 1995
$11m — My Family · 1995
$65m — Jack · 1996
$50m — The Rainmaker · 1997
Buddy · 1997
Survival On The Mountain · 1997
The Odyssey · 1997
The Florentine · 1999
$206m — Sleepy Hollow · 1999
The Third Miracle · 1999
Supernova · 2000
$10m — The Virgin Suicides · 2000
Another Day · 2001
$11m — The Legend Of Suriyothai · 2001
$59m — Jeepers Creepers · 2001
No Such Thing · 2002
CQ · 2002
Pumpkin · 2002
Assassination Tango · 2003
$63m — Jeepers Creepers 2 · 2003
$120m — Lost In Translation · 2003
$17m — Kinsey · 2004
$61m — Marie Antoinette · 2006
$99m — The Good Shepherd · 2006
Youth Without Youth · 2007
Tetro · 2009
Somewhere · 2010
$14m — Twixt · 2012
On The Road · 2012

RELOAD AND **DOUBLE** YOUR MONEY

Five movie remakes that earned double or more their cost and infinitely more than the original film.

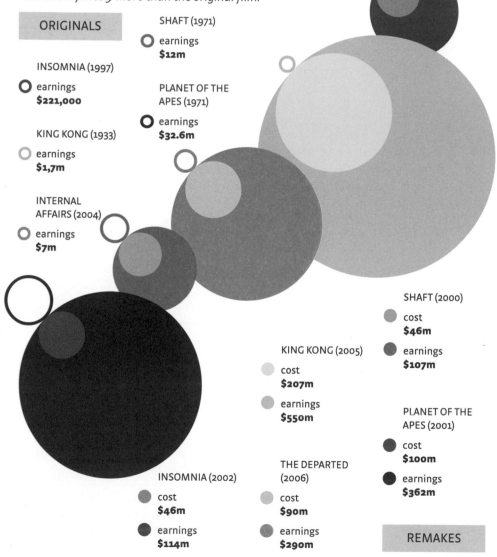

ORIGINALS

SHAFT (1971)
earnings
$12m

INSOMNIA (1997)
earnings
$221,000

PLANET OF THE APES (1971)
earnings
$32.6m

KING KONG (1933)
earnings
$1,7m

INTERNAL AFFAIRS (2004)
earnings
$7m

SHAFT (2000)
cost
$46m
earnings
$107m

KING KONG (2005)
cost
$207m
earnings
$550m

PLANET OF THE APES (2001)
cost
$100m
earnings
$362m

INSOMNIA (2002)
cost
$46m
earnings
$114m

THE DEPARTED (2006)
cost
$90m
earnings
$290m

REMAKES

CAN A ROBOT EVER BE **HUMAN?**

It's not easy to convincingly become a robot on screen, but those that do often enjoy career-defining roles (see Arnie). Here's what those actors who played such memorable robots did next.

ORIGINAL FILM

Star Trek: The Motion Picture (1979)
Android Ilia: Persis Khambatta

Galaxina (1980) Galaxina:
Dorothy Stratten

Blade Runner (1982)
Zhora: Joanna Cassidy
Rachael: Sean Young

Weird Science (1985)
Lisa: Kelly Le Brock

Aliens (1986)
Bishop: Lance Henriksen

Robocop (1987)
Robocop: Peter Weller

Robocop 2 (1990)
Robocop: Peter Weller
Robocop-2: Tom Noonan

Eve Of Destruction (1991) Eve
VIII: Renée Soutendijk

Terminator 2: Judgement Day
(1991) T-1000: Robert Patrick

Star Trek: First Contact (1996)
Borg Queen: Alice Krige

A.I. (2001) Gigolo Jane: Ashley Scott

Terminator 3: Rise Of The Machines
(2003) T-X: Kristanna Loken

I, Robot (2004) V.I.K.I.: Fiona Hogan

Serenity (2005) Leonore: Nectar Rose

TV SERIES

Falcon Crest (1982)

American Playhouse (1983)

Faerie Tale Theater (1987)

Tales From The Crypt (1992)

Dark Angel (2001-02)

TV MOVIE

*Paul Reiser Out On
A Whim* (1987)

Rainbow Drive (1990)

*The 10 Million Dollar
Getaway* (1991)

Keeper Of The City (1992)

Curse Of The Ring (2004)

*The Love Crimes Of
Gillian Guess* (2004)

FOLLOW-UP FILM

They All Laughed (1981)

Hard To Kill (1990)

Habitat (1997)

Nighthawks (1981)

The Iron Man (2006)

CINE WORLD

If the world map were redrawn to reflect the movie-going populations of different nations during a single year, this is how it would look.

#14

#2
US
1,364m

#29

#22

#5
Mexico
178m

#11

#21

#1
India
2,900m

— Rank
— Country
— Admissions

11 Brazil	112.7m	**18** Malaysia	44.1m	**25** South Africa	26.1m
12 Italy	111.2m	**19** Poland	39.2m	**26** Egypt	25.6m
13 Spain	109.5m	**20** Turkey	36.9m	**27** Taiwan	23.6m
14 Canada	108m	**21** Argentina	33.3m	**28** Belgium	22.6m
15 Australia	90.7m	**22** Netherlands	27.3m	**29** Singapore	22m
16 Philippines	65.4m	**22** Colombia	27.3m	**29** Venezuela	22m
17 Indonesia	50.1m	**24** Thailand	27.1m	**31** Hong Kong	20.1m

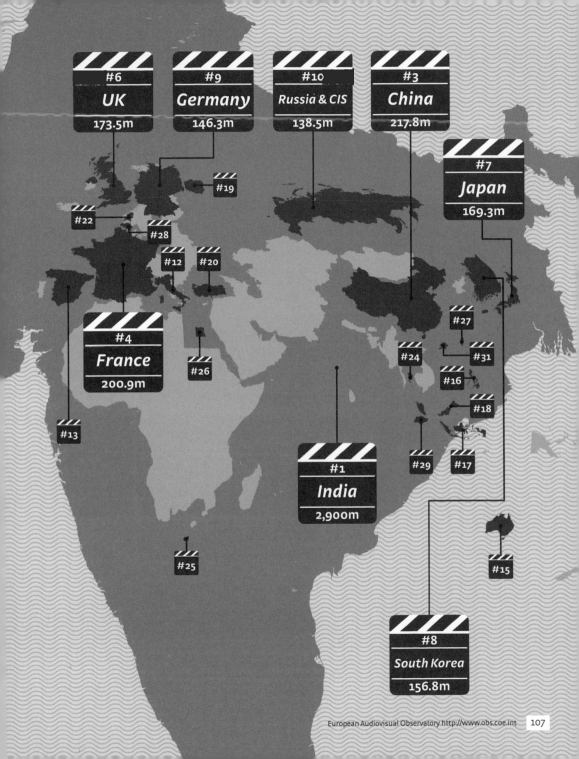

#6 UK 173.5m

#9 Germany 146.3m

#10 Russia & CIS 138.5m

#3 China 217.8m

#7 Japan 169.3m

#19

#22

#28

#12

#20

#4 France 200.9m

#26

#13

#27

#24

#31

#16

#18

#1 India 2,900m

#29

#17

#25

#15

#8 South Korea 156.8m

THE **DARK STAR** BURNS BRIGHTEST

Ever since Star Wars, space and time travel sci-fi movie franchises have searched for the source of box office greatness. Some get closer to the source than others, but nobody has been close enough to land.

$800m

The Matrix
1999–2003
$833m

Terminator
1984–2009
$819m

$850m

Back To The Future
1985–1990
$878m

$900m

Men In Black
1997–2012
$881m

$950m

Alien
1979–2012
$907m

$1b

Star Trek
1979–2009
$1.9b

● Movie franchise

✦ Franchise releases

Star Wars
1977–2008

$4.6b
Total box office

Information courtesy of Box Office Mojo and IMDb (http://www.imdb.com).
Used with permission.

HOLLYWOOD, BOLLYWOOD, BEIJING...
OR BIG MAC?

The American movie industry satisfies millions of people around the world every day, as do Big Macs. But how does America's film and most famous burger markets stack up against those of India and China?

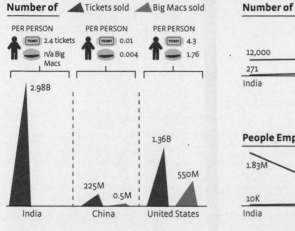

Number of ▲ Tickets sold ▲ Big Macs sold

	PER PERSON		PER PERSON		PER PERSON	
	TICKET	2.4 tickets	TICKET	0.01	TICKET	4.3
		n/a Big Macs		0.004		1.76

India: 2.98B
China: 225M, 0.5M
United States: 1.36B, 550M

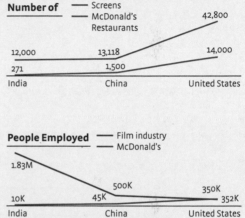

Number of — Screens — McDonald's Restaurants

	India	China	United States
Screens	12,000	13,118	42,800
			14,000
McDonald's Restaurants	271	1,500	

People Employed — Film industry — McDonald's

	India	China	United States
Film industry	1.83M	500K	350K
McDonald's	10K	45K	352K

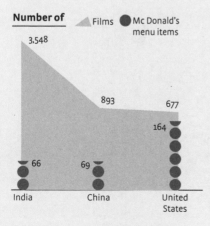

Number of ▲ Films ● Mc Donald's menu items

India: 3,548 Films, 66 menu items
China: 893 Films, 69 menu items
United States: 677 Films, 164 menu items

Average Ticket Price/Average Big Mac Price

	Ticket	Big Mac
India	$4	
China	$6.40	$2.57
United States	$8	$4.85

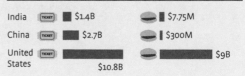

Total Box Office (2012)/McDonald's Revenue (2012)

	Box Office	Revenue
India	$1.4B	$7.75M
China	$2.7B	$300M
United States	$10.8B	$9B

THE OUTER LIMITS OF **TOM HARDY**

How, in just six moves or less, Tom Hardy can be connected with Franz Kafka, Toscanini, Andy Warhol, Thomas Hardy and a chimpanzee named Ham.

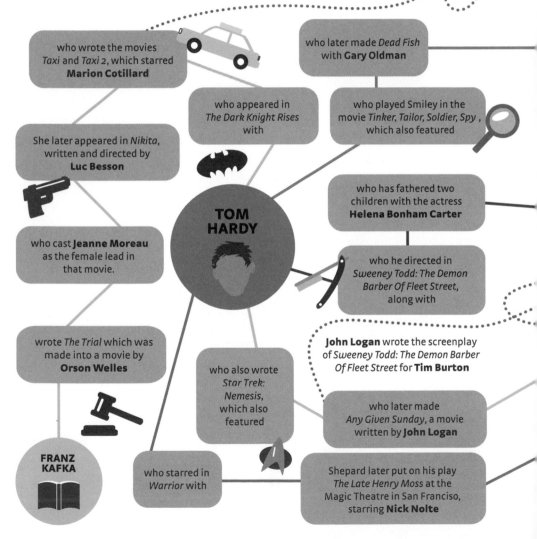

Marion Cotillard was in *Inception* with **Michael Caine**

who wrote the movies *Taxi* and *Taxi 2*, which starred **Marion Cotillard**

who later made *Dead Fish* with **Gary Oldman**

who appeared in *The Dark Knight Rises* with

who played Smiley in the movie *Tinker, Tailor, Soldier, Spy* , which also featured

She later appeared in *Nikita*, written and directed by **Luc Besson**

TOM HARDY

who has fathered two children with the actress **Helena Bonham Carter**

who cast **Jeanne Moreau** as the female lead in that movie.

who he directed in *Sweeney Todd: The Demon Barber Of Fleet Street*, along with

wrote *The Trial* which was made into a movie by **Orson Welles**

John Logan wrote the screenplay of *Sweeney Todd: The Demon Barber Of Fleet Street* for **Tim Burton**

who also wrote *Star Trek: Nemesis*, which also featured

who later made *Any Given Sunday*, a movie written by **John Logan**

FRANZ KAFKA

who starred in *Warrior* with

Shepard later put on his play *The Late Henry Moss* at the Magic Theatre in San Franciso, starring **Nick Nolte**

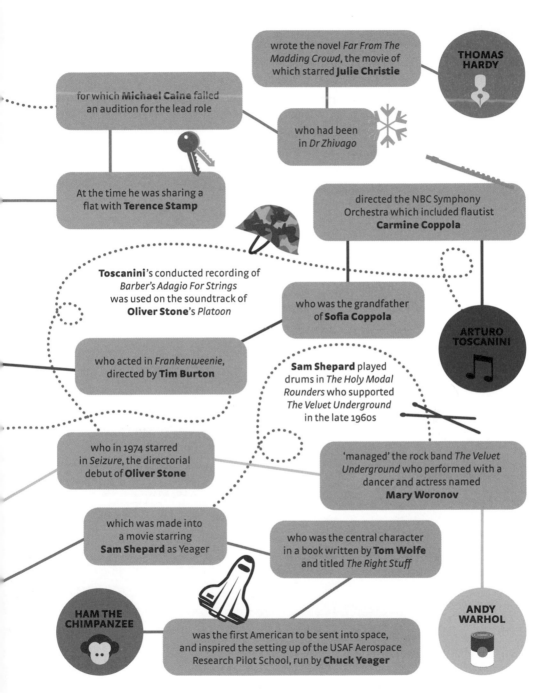

wrote the novel *Far From The Madding Crowd*, the movie of which starred **Julie Christie**

THOMAS HARDY

for which **Michael Caine** failed an audition for the lead role

who had been in *Dr Zhivago*

At the time he was sharing a flat with **Terence Stamp**

directed the NBC Symphony Orchestra which included flautist **Carmine Coppola**

Toscanini's conducted recording of *Barber's Adagio For Strings* was used on the soundtrack of **Oliver Stone**'s *Platoon*

who was the grandfather of **Sofia Coppola**

ARTURO TOSCANINI

who acted in *Frankenweenie*, directed by **Tim Burton**

Sam Shepard played drums in *The Holy Modal Rounders* who supported *The Velvet Underground* in the late 1960s

who in 1974 starred in *Seizure*, the directorial debut of **Oliver Stone**

'managed' the rock band *The Velvet Underground* who performed with a dancer and actress named **Mary Woronov**

which was made into a movie starring **Sam Shepard** as Yeager

who was the central character in a book written by **Tom Wolfe** and titled *The Right Stuff*

HAM THE CHIMPANZEE

ANDY WARHOL

was the first American to be sent into space, and inspired the setting up of the USAF Aerospace Research Pilot School, run by **Chuck Yeager**

THE **TITANIC** MONEY SHOT

Every truly memorable movie contains at least one truly memorable and important scene that lingers in the audience's memory. That memorable scene has to contain certain elements in order for it to work. Here's a breakdown of the 'flying' scene in Titanic and what makes it so powerful.

Post-Production
Intercut close-ups that fill the screen with two people in love, who trust one another and are oblivious to impending danger. Remind the viewer of the danger by intercutting shots of the sea, just as the fog creeps in on Bogart and Bergman in the farewell scene of *Casablanca* (1942)
5 major editing awards

Speed
Layer whistling wind over cross-bow swooping camera shots, changing perspective and creating the impression of motion to give a sense of boundless progression toward a fatal destiny, similar to Celia Johnson's rush to the train in the final scene of *Brief Encounter* (1945)
Won 8 best sound and production design awards

Emotion

Demand a range of emotions from both actors, at first restrained and then daring, with hesitancy changing swiftly to trust and elation. Just as O'Neal and McGraw move from anger through denial and disbelief to love in the proposal scene in *Love Story* (1970)
Won 6 major actor and actress awards

Colour

Mix saturated, bold colours of a sunset that envelopes Jack and Rose to a level of unreality and renders it as erotically charged as the deep red sunset that illuminates the first kiss scene between Rhett and Scarlett in *Gone With The Wind* (1939)
Won 9 cinematography and art direction awards

Composition

Create a sense of enormous scale, movement, emotion, progression and impending doom to contrast with the blithe hope and love of the lead characters who are as doomed as Beatty and Dunaway's *Bonnie And Clyde* (1967)
Won 27 best director and best picture awards

Synchronization

Clothe the two lead characters to show the difference in their social and economic positions, make them symbolic of the inverted power balance between them (she is superior to him). Balancing the pair on the prow of the ship reverses the power relationship just as in *The Bodyguard* (1992) when the pop star is carried to safety by her bouncer.
4 awards for effects and costume design

Music

Layer rising and falling lush symphonic strings that are romantic and elegaic, just as in the famous cigarette lighting scene of *Now Voyager* (1942)
14 major awards

LOVE LINES OF **PARIS**

This map of the Paris Metro shows the locations in which beautiful creatures have been sought and chased in hit movies over six decades and the location of key scenes from each movie.

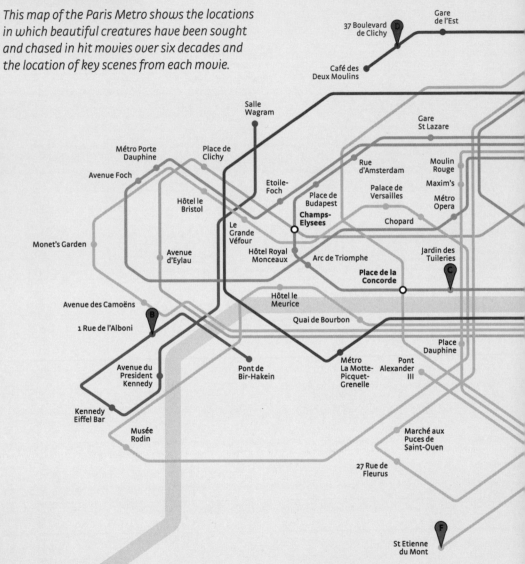

Gare de l'Est

37 Boulevard de Clichy

Café des Deux Moulins

Salle Wagram

Gare St Lazare

Métro Porte Dauphine

Place de Clichy

Avenue Foch

Rue d'Amsterdam

Moulin Rouge

Maxim's

Hôtel le Bristol

Etoile-Foch

Place de Budapest

Palace de Versailles

Métro Opera

Champs-Elysees

Le Grande Véfour

Hôtel Royal Monceaux

Chopard

Monet's Garden

Avenue d'Eylau

Arc de Triomphe

Jardin des Tuileries

Place de la Concorde

Avenue des Camoëns

Hôtel le Meurice

1 Rue de l'Alboni

Quai de Bourbon

Place Dauphine

Avenue du President Kennedy

Pont de Bir-Hakein

Métro La Motte-Picquet-Grenelle

Pont Alexander III

Kennedy Eiffel Bar

Musée Rodin

Marché aux Puces de Saint-Ouen

27 Rue de Fleurus

St Etienne du Mont

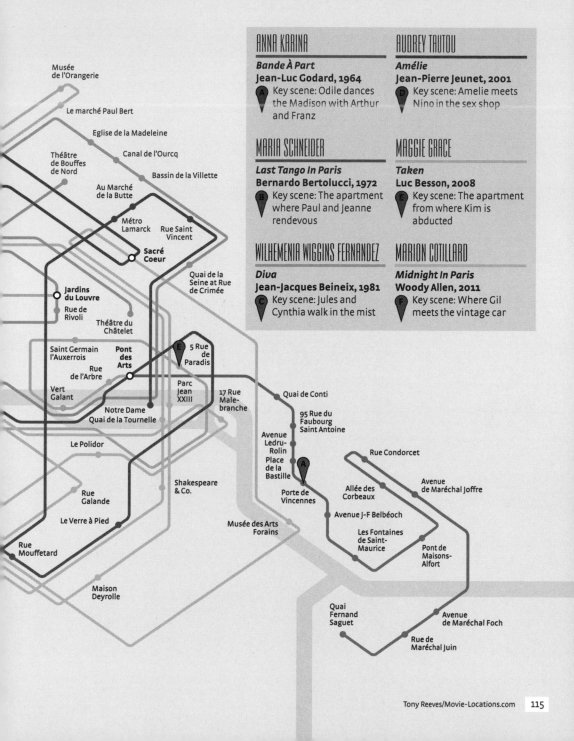

BRUCE WILLIS DIES HARD

As New York police detective John McLane, Bruce Willis survives countless gunfights, fistfights, attempted stabbings and explosions over the course of five Die Hard movies. However, over the course of his acting career, he's been 'killed' 13 times.

BRUCE WILLIS ON-SCREEN DEATHS

- Drowned
- Slashed Throat
- Shot
- Nuked
- Old age

Charlie's Angels Full Throttle (2003) Shot in the head

Grindhouse: Planet Terror (2007) Shot after being infected by zombie virus

 Billy Bathgate (1991) Drowned by the Mafia

Mortal Thoughts (1991) Throat slashed with a Stanley knife

The Jackal (1997) Shot by a female Basque terrorist

Hart's War (2002) Shot by Nazi POW camp commander

Twelve Monkeys (1995) Shot by policeman) – but younger self watches

Sin City (2005) Shot in the back

The Sixth Sense (1999) Shot in the stomach by a psychiatric patient

The Cold Light Of Day (2012) Shot in the back by a sniper

Looper (2013) Having time-travelled back in time, his 'younger self' shoots him, thus erasing the future Bruce

Armageddon (1998) Nukes himself deliberately

Death Becomes Her (1992) Old age

BOYS WILL BE GIRLS & GIRLS WILL BE BOYS

The most successful cross-dressing movies of all time revealed.

$441m – Robin Williams in *Mrs Doubtfire* (1993)

$200m – Dustin Hoffman in *Tootsie* (1982)

$39m – Julie Andrews in *Victor / Victoria* (1982)

$60m – Barbra Streisand in *Yentl* (1983)

$289m – Gwyneth Paltrow in *Shakespeare In Love* (1998)

$22m – Michel Serrault in *La Cage Aux Folles* (1978)

$25m – Jack Lemmon and Tony Curtis in *Some Like It Hot* (1959)

$30m – Guy Pearce, Terence Stamp, and Hugo Weaving in *The Adventures Of Priscilla, Queen Of The Desert* (1994)

$174m – Martin Lawrence in *Big Momma's House* (2000)

$138m – Martin Lawrence in *Big Momma's House 2* (2006)

$100m – Jaye Davidson in *The Crying Game* (1992)

$83m – Martin Lawrence and Brandon T Jackson in *Big Momma's: Like Father Like Son* (2011)

$113m – Tim Curry *The Rocky Horror Picture Show* (1975)

$32m – Michael Caine in *Dressed To Kill* (1980)

$113m – Shawn and Marlon Wayans in *White Chicks* (2004)

- ■ Male to female
- ■ Female to male
- ■ Female to male to female

SEVEN STORIES WE ALL KNOW

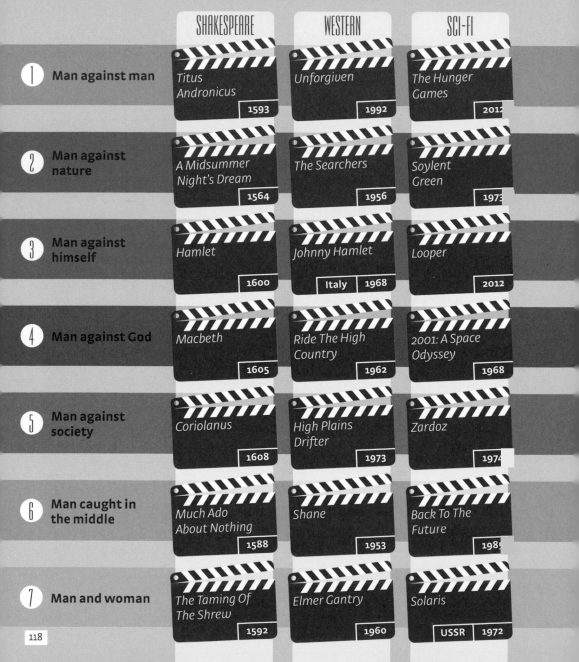

		SHAKESPEARE	WESTERN	SCI-FI
1	Man against man	*Titus Andronicus* — 1593	*Unforgiven* — 1992	*The Hunger Games* — 2012
2	Man against nature	*A Midsummer Night's Dream* — 1564	*The Searchers* — 1956	*Soylent Green* — 1973
3	Man against himself	*Hamlet* — 1600	*Johnny Hamlet* — Italy 1968	*Looper* — 2012
4	Man against God	*Macbeth* — 1605	*Ride The High Country* — 1962	*2001: A Space Odyssey* — 1968
5	Man against society	*Coriolanus* — 1608	*High Plains Drifter* — 1973	*Zardoz* — 1974
6	Man caught in the middle	*Much Ado About Nothing* — 1588	*Shane* — 1953	*Back To The Future* — 1985
7	Man and woman	*The Taming Of The Shrew* — 1592	*Elmer Gantry* — 1960	*Solaris* — USSR 1972

There are only seven stories, claimed Sir Arthur Quiller-Couch, and they're all conflicts. Here's how Shakespeare and different movie genres play them.

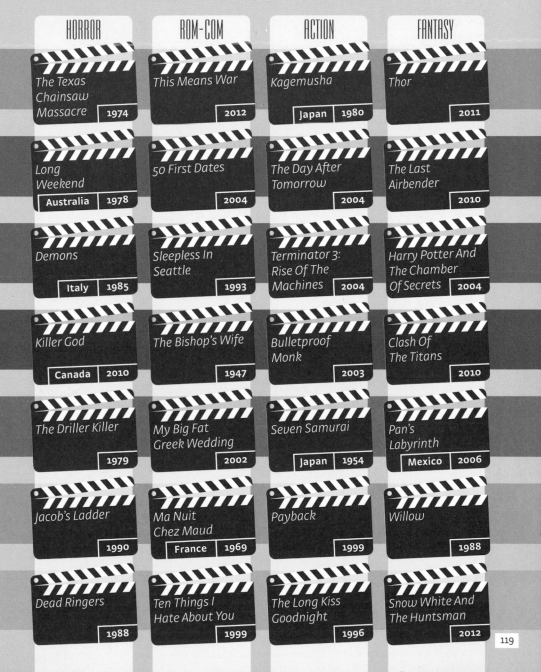

HORROR

The Texas Chainsaw Massacre — 1974

Long Weekend — Australia — 1978

Demons — Italy — 1985

Killer God — Canada — 2010

The Driller Killer — 1979

Jacob's Ladder — 1990

Dead Ringers — 1988

ROM-COM

This Means War — 2012

50 First Dates — 2004

Sleepless In Seattle — 1993

The Bishop's Wife — 1947

My Big Fat Greek Wedding — 2002

Ma Nuit Chez Maud — France — 1969

Ten Things I Hate About You — 1999

ACTION

Kagemusha — Japan — 1980

The Day After Tomorrow — 2004

Terminator 3: Rise Of The Machines — 2004

Bulletproof Monk — 2003

Seven Samurai — Japan — 1954

Payback — 1999

The Long Kiss Goodnight — 1996

FANTASY

Thor — 2011

The Last Airbender — 2010

Harry Potter And The Chamber Of Secrets — 2004

Clash Of The Titans — 2010

Pan's Labyrinth — Mexico — 2006

Willow — 1988

Snow White And The Huntsman — 2012

THE BOURNE CLOCK

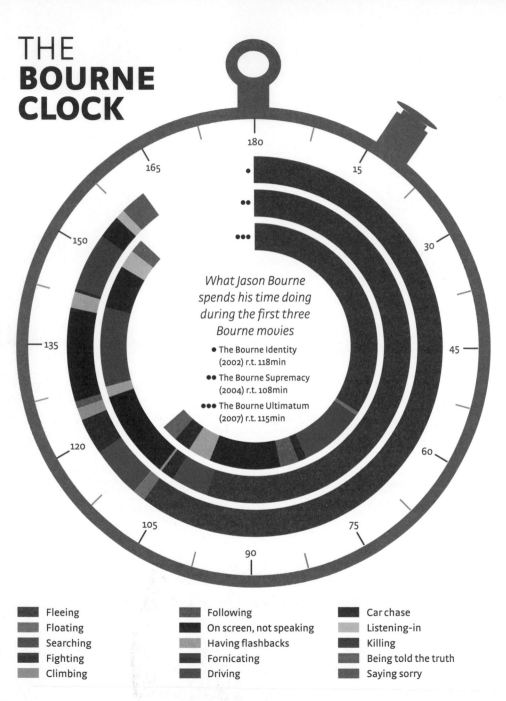

What Jason Bourne spends his time doing during the first three Bourne movies

- ● The Bourne Identity (2002) r.t. 118min
- ●● The Bourne Supremacy (2004) r.t. 108min
- ●●● The Bourne Ultimatum (2007) r.t. 115min

Legend:
- Fleeing
- Floating
- Searching
- Fighting
- Climbing
- Following
- On screen, not speaking
- Having flashbacks
- Fornicating
- Driving
- Car chase
- Listening-in
- Killing
- Being told the truth
- Saying sorry

IT SHOULD HAVE BEEN **ME**, TOO

The American Academy Award for best foreign language film has not always been given to the most well-regarded work. These winners are contrasted with the movies that, in the opinion of the critics (according to Rottentomatoes.com), should have won the Oscar.

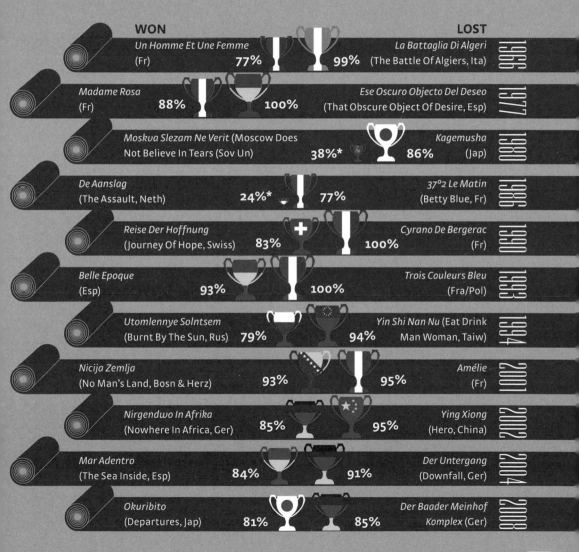

WON				LOST	
Un Homme Et Une Femme (Fr)	77%	99%		La Battaglia Di Algeri (The Battle Of Algiers, Ita)	1966
Madame Rosa (Fr)	88%	100%		Ese Oscuro Objecto Del Deseo (That Obscure Object Of Desire, Esp)	1977
Moskva Slezam Ne Verit (Moscow Does Not Believe In Tears (Sov Un)	38%*	86%		Kagemusha (Jap)	1980
De Aanslag (The Assault, Neth)	24%*	77%		37°2 Le Matin (Betty Blue, Fr)	1986
Reise Der Hoffnung (Journey Of Hope, Swiss)	83%	100%		Cyrano De Bergerac (Fr)	1990
Belle Epoque (Esp)	93%	100%		Trois Couleurs Bleu (Fra/Pol)	1993
Utomlennye Solntsem (Burnt By The Sun, Rus)	79%	94%		Yin Shi Nan Nu (Eat Drink Man Woman, Taiw)	1994
Nicija Zemlja (No Man's Land, Bosn & Herz)	93%	95%		Amélie (Fr)	2001
Nirgendwo In Afrika (Nowhere In Africa, Ger)	85%	95%		Ying Xiong (Hero, China)	2002
Mar Adentro (The Sea Inside, Esp)	84%	91%		Der Untergang (Downfall, Ger)	2004
Okuribito (Departures, Jap)	81%	85%		Der Baader Meinhof Komplex (Ger)	2008

* score of rottentomatoes.com users because no critic rating available.

The Grey - AK

Back To The Future II - CA

Back To The Future - CA

Constantine - CA

Poltergeist - CA

Psycho - CA

Blade Runner - CA

Fargo - ND

Unforgiven - WY

Identity - NV

The Shining - CO

Citizen Kane - CO

Point Break - CA

Night Of The Twisters - NB

Planes, Trains And Automobiles - KS

500 MPH Storm - NM

Tornado - TX

Rain

Thunder and Lightning

Snow

Tornado

BAD WEATHER **STARTS PLAY**

The top 40 American bad weather movies of all time.

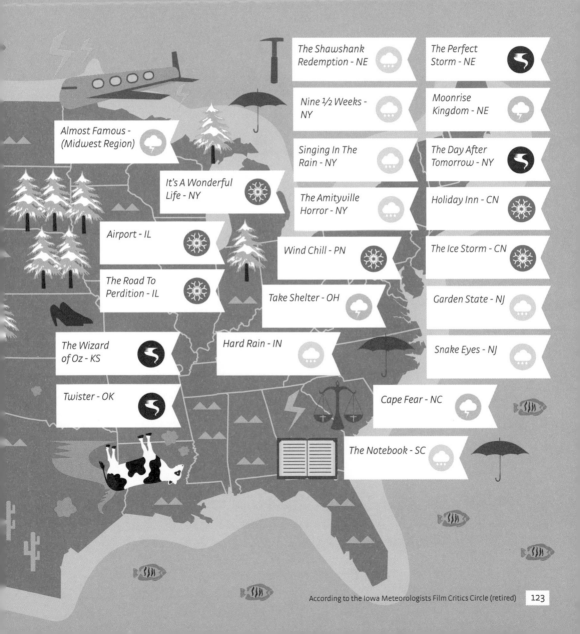

Almost Famous - (Midwest Region)

It's A Wonderful Life - NY

Airport - IL

The Road To Perdition - IL

The Wizard of Oz - KS

Twister - OK

The Shawshank Redemption - NE

Nine ½ Weeks - NY

Singing In The Rain - NY

The Amityville Horror - NY

Wind Chill - PN

Take Shelter - OH

Hard Rain - IN

The Perfect Storm - NE

Moonrise Kingdom - NE

The Day After Tomorrow - NY

Holiday Inn - CN

The Ice Storm - CN

Garden State - NJ

Snake Eyes - NJ

Cape Fear - NC

The Notebook - SC

NO **LAUGHING** MATTER?

At the end of the 85th Annual Academy Awards in Hollywood the number of comedy films to have won the coveted Best Picture award stood at 12. Other Academy Awards have been given for comedy direction, scripts and roles, but they've often been spread thinly and far apart.

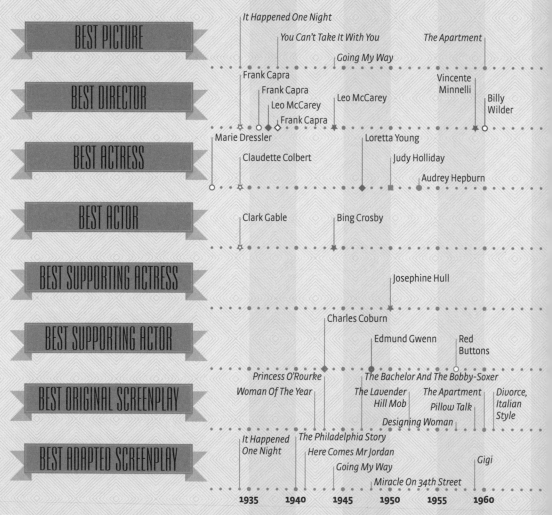

BEST PICTURE
- It Happened One Night
- You Can't Take It With You
- Going My Way
- The Apartment

BEST DIRECTOR
- Frank Capra
- Frank Capra
- Leo McCarey
- Frank Capra
- Leo McCarey
- Vincente Minnelli
- Billy Wilder

BEST ACTRESS
- Marie Dressler
- Claudette Colbert
- Loretta Young
- Judy Holliday
- Audrey Hepburn

BEST ACTOR
- Clark Gable
- Bing Crosby

BEST SUPPORTING ACTRESS
- Josephine Hull

BEST SUPPORTING ACTOR
- Charles Coburn
- Edmund Gwenn
- Red Buttons

BEST ORIGINAL SCREENPLAY
- Princess O'Rourke
- Woman Of The Year
- The Bachelor And The Bobby-Soxer
- The Lavender Hill Mob
- The Apartment
- Pillow Talk
- Designing Woman
- Divorce, Italian Style

BEST ADAPTED SCREENPLAY
- It Happened One Night
- The Philadelphia Story
- Here Comes Mr Jordan
- Going My Way
- Miracle On 34th Street
- Gigi

1935 1940 1945 1950 1955 1960

KEY TO FILMS

- ■ A Fish Called Wanda
- ■ A Thousand Clowns
- □ Annie Hall
- ■ As Good As It Gets
- □ Being There
- ■ Born Yesterday
- □ Bullets Over Broadway
- ■ Cactus Flower
- □ California Suite
- ■ City Slickers
- □ Driving Miss Daisy

- ✦ Ed Wood
- ✦ Gigi
- ✦ Going My Way
- ✦ Hannah And Her Sisters
- ✦ Harvey
- ✦ It Happened One Night
- ✦ Life Is Beautiful
- ✦ Little Miss Sunshine
- ✦ Mary Poppins
- ✦ M*A*S*H
- ✦ Melvin And Howard
- ✦ Mighty Aphrodite

- ○ Min And Bill
- ● Miracle On 34th Street
- ○ Moonstruck
- ○ Mr Deeds Goes To Town
- ● My Cousin Vinny
- ○ Prizzi's Honor
- ■ Roman Holiday
- ○ Sayonara
- ● Shakespeare In Love
- ○ Silver Linings Playbook
- ● Terms Of Endearment
- ○ The Apartment

- ◇ The Artist
- ◆ The Awful Truth
- ◆ The Farmer's Daughter
- ◆ The Fortune Cookie
- ◆ The More The Merrier
- ◇ The Sting
- ◆ The Sunshine Boys
- ◇ Tom Jones
- ◆ Tootsie
- ◇ Topkapi
- ◆ Vicky Cristina Barcelona
- ◇ You Can't Take It With You

Tom Jones | The Sting | Terms Of Endearment | Shakespeare In Love

Annie Hall | Driving Miss Daisy | The Artist

George Roy Hill

Tony Richardson | Woody Allen | James L. Brooks | Michael Hazanavicius

Shirley MacLaine | Helen Hunt

Julie Andrews | Diane Keaton | Cher | Gwyneth Paltrow

Jessica Tandy | Jennifer Lawrence

Roberto Benigni | Jean Dujardin

Mary Steenburgen | Anjelica Huston | Marisa Tomei

Maggie Smith | Jessica Lange | Dianne Wiest | Dianne Wiest

Olympia Dukakis | Mira Sorvino | Penélope Cruz

Goldie Hawn | Judi Dench

Peter Ustinov | George Burns | Michael Caine | Alan Arkin

Kevin Kline

Melvyn Douglas | Jack Palance

Walter Matthau | Martin Landau

Father Goose | Annie Hall | Hannah And Her Sisters | Midnight In Paris

The Producers | Breaking Away | Shakespeare In Love | Little Miss Sunshine

The Hospital | Melvin And Howard | Moonstruck | Juno

The Sating

Terms of Endearment

Tom Jones | M*A*S*H | Driving Miss Daisy | Sideways

1965 | 1970 | 1975 | 1980 | 1985 | 1990 | 1995 | 2000 | 2005 | 2010

All films identified primarily as comedy by IMDb.com

MIND THE **AGE GAP**

Actors reach their peak in different tongues, according to this data which uses the top ten highest grossing movies in the English, French and Spanish languages.

30

43.6

32

1 AVATAR			
2009	Sam Worthington		32
2 TITANIC			
1997	Leonardo DiCaprio		23
3 THE AVENGERS			
2012	Chris Evans		30
4 HARRY POTTER & THE DEATHLY HALLOWS PART 2			
2011	Daniel Radcliffe		21
5 TRANSFORMERS: DARK OF THE MOON			
2011	Shia LaBeouf		24
6 LORD OF THE RINGS: THE RETURN OF THE KING			
2003	Elijah Wood		21
7 SKYFALL			
2012	Daniel Craig		43
8 THE DARK KNIGHT RISES			
2012	Christian Bale		37
9 PIRATES OF THE CARIBBEAN: DEAD MAN'S CHEST			
2006	Johnny Depp		42
10 STAR WARS: EPISODE 1 THE PHANTOM MENACE			
1999	Ewan McGregor		26

1 INTOUCHABLES			
2011	Omar Sy		32
2 BIENVENUE CHEZ LES CH'TIS			
2008	Kad Merad		43
3 AMELIE			
2001	Mathieu Kassovitz		33
4 THE ARTIST			
2011	Jean Dujardin		38
5 ASTERIX AND OBELISK: MISSION CLEOPATRE			
2002	Gérard Depardieu		53
6 LA VIE EN ROSE			
2007	Jean-Pierre Martins		35
7 LE PACTE DES LOUPS			
2001	Samuel Le Bihan		35
8 LA GRANDE VADROUILLE			
1996	Bourvil		35
9 DES HOMMES ET DES DIEUX			
2010	Lambert Wilson		51
10 AMOUR			
2012	Jean-Louis Trintignant		81

1 VOLVER			
2006	n/a		n/a
2 EL LABERINTO DEL FAUNO			
2006	Doug Jones		35
3 EL ORFANATO			
2007	Fernando Cayo		38
4 TODO SOBRE MI MADRE			
1999	Eloy Azorín		21
5 DIARIOS DE MOTOCICLETA			
2004	Gael Garcia Bernal		25
6 HABLE CON ELLA			
2002	Javier Cámara		34
7 EL SECRETO SE SUS OJOS			
2009	Ricardo Darín		51
8 Y TU MAMA TAMBIEN			
2001	Gael Garcia Bernal		22
9 BIUTIFUL			
2011	Javier Bardem		41
10 COMO AGUA PARA CHOCOLATE			
1992	Marco Leonardi		23

1 Movie rank | ■ Year of release | ■ Leading male | ■ Leading female | ■ Age | ▲ Average age

■■ **English** language | ■■ **French** language | ■■ **Spanish** language

29 | 37.6 | 34.3

1 AVATAR		
■ 2009	■ Zoe Saldana	■ 30

2 TITANIC		
■ 1997	■ Kate Winslet	■ 22

3 THE AVENGERS		
■ 2012	■ Scarlett Johansson	■ 27

4 HARRY POTTER & THE DEATHLY HALLOWS PART 2		
■ 2011	■ Emma Watson	■ 20

5 TRANSFORMERS: DARK OF THE MOON		
■ 2011	■ Rosie Huntington Whitely	■ 32

6 LORD OF THE RINGS: THE RETURN OF THE KING		
■ 2003	■ Cate Blanchett	■ 32

7 SKYFALL		
■ 2012	■ Judi Dench	■ 77

8 THE DARK KNIGHT RISES		
■ 2012	■ Anne Hathaway	■ 29

9 PIRATES OF THE CARIBBEAN: DEAD MAN'S CHEST		
■ 2006	■ Keira Knightley	■ 20

10 STAR WARS: EPISODE 1 THE PHANTOM MENACE		
■ 1999	■ Natalie Portman	■ 17

1 INTOUCHABLES		
■ 2011	■ Audrey Fleurot	■ 32

2 BIENVENUE CHEZ LES CH'TIS		
■ 2008	■ Zoé Félix	■ 31

3 AMELIE		
■ 2001	■ Audrey Tautou	■ 24

4 THE ARTIST		
■ 2011	■ Bérénice Bejo	■ 34

5 ASTERIX AND OBELISK: MISSION CLEOPATRE		
■ 2002	■ Monica Bellucci	■ 37

6 LA VIE EN ROSE		
■ 2007	■ Marion Cotillard	■ 35

7 LE PACTE DES LOUPS		
■ 2001	■ Emelie Dequenne	■ 20

8 LA GRANDE VADROUILLE		
■ 1996	■ Andréa Parisy	■ 60

9 DES HOMMES ET DES DIEUX		
■ 2010	■ Sabrina Ouazani	■ 19

10 AMOUR		
■ 2012	■ Emmanuelle Riva	■ 84

1 VOLVER		
■ 2006	■ Penélope Cruz	■ 31

2 EL LABERINTO DEL FAUNO		
■ 2006	■ Ivana Baquero	■ 12

4 EL ORFANATO		
■ 2007	■ Belén Rueda	■ 41

4 TODO SOBRE MI MADRE		
■ 1999	■ Cecilia Roth	■ 42

5 DIARIOS DE MOTOCICLETA		
■ 2004	■ Mercedes Morán	■ 48

6 HABLE CON ELLA		
■ 2002	■ Rosario Flores	■ 38

7 EL SECRETO SE SUS OJOS		
■ 2009	■ Soledad Villamil	■ 39

8 Y TU MAMA TAMBIEN		
■ 2001	■ Maribel Verdú	■ 30

9 BIUTIFUL		
■ 2011	■ Maricel Alvarez	■ 40

10 COMO AGUA PARA CHOCOLATE		
■ 1992	■ Lumi Cavazos	■ 23

Information courtesy of Box Office Mojo and IMDb (http://www.imdb.com). Used with permission.

THE **BOND** UNIVERSE (PART 1)

Ian Fleming's international espionage agent 007 has travelled the world in order to save us from destructive egomaniacs. These are the routes taken by the first three actors to play James Bond in each of their movies.

(outer space)

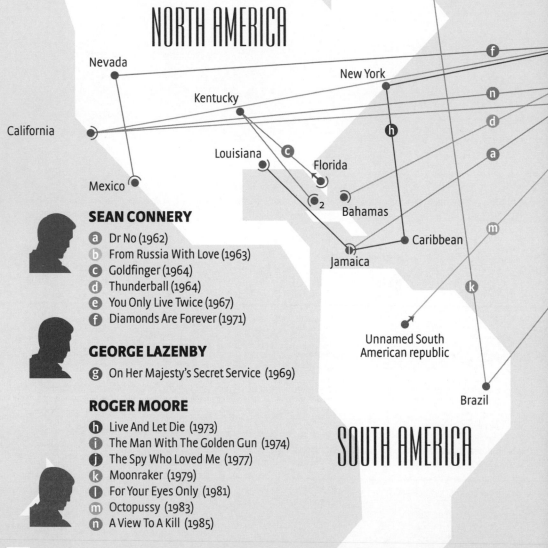

NORTH AMERICA

Nevada

New York

Kentucky

California

Louisiana

Florida

Mexico

2

Bahamas

Caribbean

Jamaica

SEAN CONNERY

- ⓐ Dr No (1962)
- ⓑ From Russia With Love (1963)
- ⓒ Goldfinger (1964)
- ⓓ Thunderball (1964)
- ⓔ You Only Live Twice (1967)
- ⓕ Diamonds Are Forever (1971)

GEORGE LAZENBY

- ⓖ On Her Majesty's Secret Service (1969)

ROGER MOORE

- ⓗ Live And Let Die (1973)
- ⓘ The Man With The Golden Gun (1974)
- ⓙ The Spy Who Loved Me (1977)
- ⓚ Moonraker (1979)
- ⓛ For Your Eyes Only (1981)
- ⓜ Octopussy (1983)
- ⓝ A View To A Kill (1985)

Unnamed South American republic

Brazil

SOUTH AMERICA

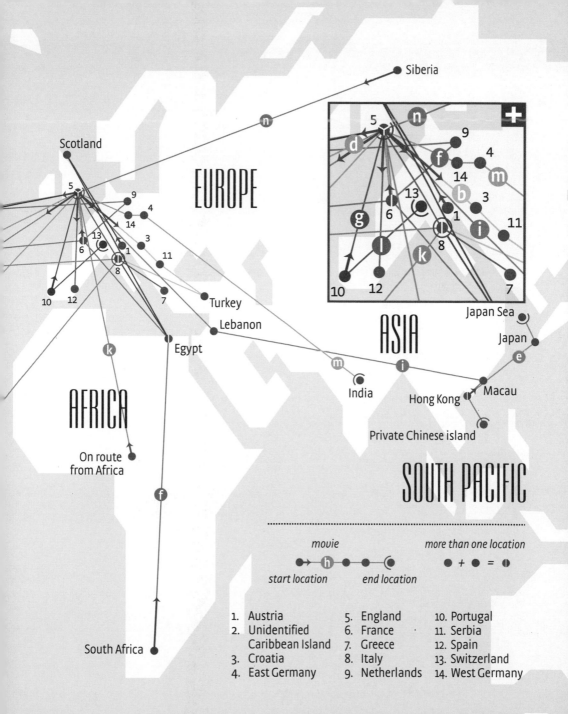

Siberia

Scotland

EUROPE

ASIA

AFRICA

Turkey

Lebanon

Egypt

On route
from Africa

Japan Sea

Japan

Macau

Hong Kong

India

Private Chinese island

South Africa

SOUTH PACIFIC

movie

start location — *end location*

more than one location

● + ● = ◖

1. Austria
2. Unidentified Caribbean Island
3. Croatia
4. East Germany
5. England
6. France
7. Greece
8. Italy
9. Netherlands
10. Portugal
11. Serbia
12. Spain
13. Switzerland
14. West Germany

THE **BOND** UNIVERSE (PART 2)

Ian Fleming's international espionage agent 007 has travelled the world in order to save us from destructive egomaniacs. These are the routes taken by the last three actors to play James Bond in each of their movies.

NORTH AMERICA

Florida

ⓖ

3

ⓒ

5

ⓕ

Cuba   10

ⓑ

Fictional republic
of Isthmus

SOUTH AMERICA

ⓗ

Bolivia

TIMOTHY DALTON
ⓐ The Living Daylights (1987)
ⓑ Licence To Kill (1989)

PIERCE BROSNAN
ⓒ GoldenEye (1995)
ⓓ Tomorrow Never Dies (1997)
ⓔ The World Is Not Enough (1999)
ⓕ Die Another Day (2002)

DANIEL CRAIG
ⓖ Casino Royale (2006)
ⓗ Quantum Of Solace (2008)
ⓘ Skyfall (2012)

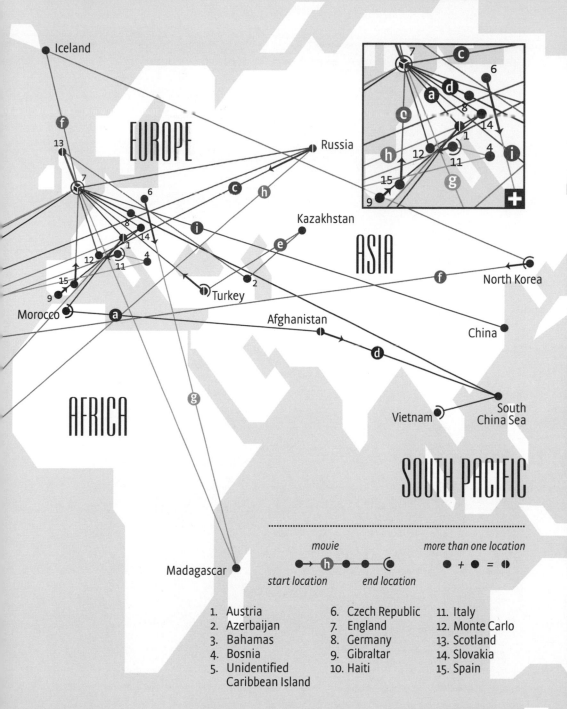

Iceland

EUROPE

Russia

Kazakhstan

ASIA

North Korea

China

Turkey

Afghanistan

Morocco

Vietnam

South China Sea

AFRICA

SOUTH PACIFIC

Madagascar

movie

start location   end location

more than one location

● + ● = ◖

1. Austria
2. Azerbaijan
3. Bahamas
4. Bosnia
5. Unidentified Caribbean Island
6. Czech Republic
7. England
8. Germany
9. Gibraltar
10. Haiti
11. Italy
12. Monte Carlo
13. Scotland
14. Slovakia
15. Spain

NAME THAT BOOK

Identify these movies adapted from literature. The first letter of the title is included to help you identify each one.

LEADING **MAN**

The composite perfect leading man according to a panel of (female) critics would look like this.

Skull
Will Smith
I Am Legend, 2007
$585m

Eyes
Robert Pattinson
The Twilight Saga: Eclipse, 2010
$698m

Nose
Liam Neeson
Clash Of The Titans, 2010
$493m

Cheeks
Brad Pitt
Mr & Mrs Smith, 2005
$478m

Lips
Javier Bardem
Skyfall, 2012
$950m

Hair
Johnny Depp
Pirates Of The Caribbean: On Stranger Tides, 2011
$1.044b

Forehead
Leonardo DiCaprio
Inception, 2010
$825.5m

Eyebrows
Colin Farrell
Minority Report, 2002
$358m

Ears
Hugh Jackman
X-Men: The Last Stand, 2006
$459m

Facial hair
Idris Elba
Prometheus, 2012
$402.5m

Teeth
Tom Cruise
War Of The Worlds, 2005
$592m

Chin
George Clooney
Ocean's Eleven, 2001
$451m

Information courtesy of Box Office Mojo.
Used with permission.

A WOMAN'S **WORK**

Studios are reluctant to give women the job of directing a movie, so it helps if you're already a famous actress who can also produce, write, or make music.

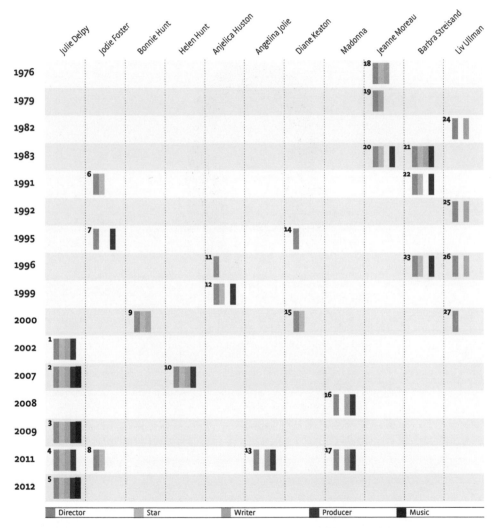

Director | Star | Writer | Producer | Music

1 Looking For Jimmy | **2** 2 Days In Paris | **3** The Countess | **4** Le Skylab | **5** 2 Days In New York | **6** Little Man Tate | **7** Home For The Holidays **8** The Beaver | **9** Return To Me | **10** Then She Found Me | **11** Bastard Out Of Carolina | **12** Agnes Brown | **13** In The Land Of Blood And Honey **14** Unstrung Heroes | **15** Hanging Up | **16** Filth And Wisdom | **17** W.E. | **18** Lumière | **19** L'Adolescente | **20** Lillian Gish | **21** Yentl | **22** The Prince Of Tides | **23** The Mirror Has Two Faces | **24** 'Parting' segment of Love | **25** Sofie | **26** Kristin Lavransdatter | **27** Faithless

ALL CREATURES **GREAT** AND **SMALL**

Animated and animal movies have become incredibly successful in getting the modern family into the cinema. The box office for the most successful of their genre (according to boxofficemojo.com) isn't always reflected in their audience ratings though (according to rottentomatoes.com).

Shrek 2
TOP MOVIE IN **FANTASY FIGURES** GENRE

91%
$1.06 billions

Toy Story
TOP MOVIE IN **TOYS COME TO LIFE** GENRE

80%
Eight Below
TOP MOVIE IN **FAMILY ANIMAL** GENRE

$120 millions

Seabiscuit
TOP MOVIE IN **HORSE** GENRE

74%
$148 millions

69%
$920 millions

83%
$915 millions

Jurassic Park
TOP MOVIE IN **CREATURE FEATURE** GENRE

$225 millions
53%

Chicken Run
TOP MOVIE IN **STOP MOTION** GENRE

$274 millions
49%

Scooby Doo
TOP MOVIE IN **DOG** GENRE

$623 millions
84%

Ratatouille
TOP MOVIE IN **MOUSE/RAT** GENRE

$308 millions
65%

The Polar Express
TOP MOVIE IN **MOTION CAPTURE** GENRE

rottentomatoes.com Ratings

STUDIOS
- Disney/Pixar
- Walt Disney Pictures
- DreamWorks
- Warner Bros
- Fox 2000
- Universal

Alvin And The Chipmunks
TOP MOVIE IN **TALKING ANIMALS** GENRE

$443 millions
59%

WALL-E
TOP MOVIE IN **SCI-FI ROBOT** GENRE

89%
$521 millions

How to Train Your Dragon
TOP MOVIE IN **DRAGONS** GENRE

90%
$495 millions

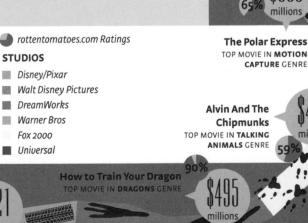

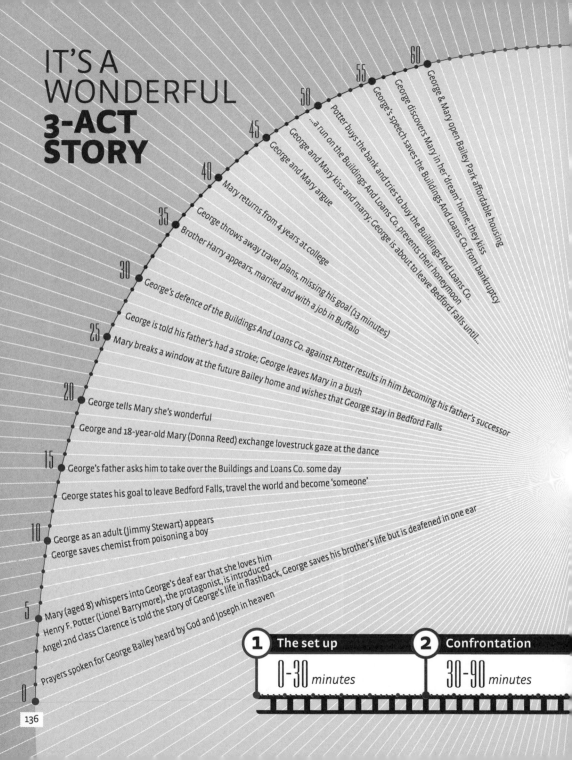

IT'S A WONDERFUL
3-ACT
STORY

60 — George & Mary open Bailey Park affordable housing

George discovers Mary in her 'dream' home; they kiss

55 — George's speech saves the Buildings And Loans Co. from bankruptcy

50 — Potter buys the bank and tries to buy the Buildings And Loans Co.

...a run on the Buildings And Loans Co. prevents their honeymoon

45 — George and Mary kiss and marry. George is about to leave Bedford Falls until...

George and Mary argue

40 —

Mary returns from 4 years at college

35 — George throws away travel plans, missing his goal (13 minutes)

Brother Harry appears, married and with a job in Buffalo

30 — George's defence of the Buildings And Loans Co. against Potter results in him becoming his father's successor

25 — George is told his father's had a stroke; George leaves Mary in a bush

Mary breaks a window at the future Bailey home and wishes that George stay in Bedford Falls

20 — George tells Mary she's wonderful

George and 18-year-old Mary (Donna Reed) exchange lovestruck gaze at the dance

15 — George's father asks him to take over the Buildings and Loans Co. some day

George states his goal to leave Bedford Falls, travel the world and become 'someone'

10 — George as an adult (Jimmy Stewart) appears

George saves chemist from poisoning a boy

George saves his brother's life but is deafened in one ear

5 — Mary (aged 8) whispers into George's deaf ear that she loves him

Henry F. Potter (Lionel Barrymore), the protagonist, is introduced

Angel 2nd class Clarence is told the story of George's life in flashback,

Prayers spoken for George Bailey heard by God and Joseph in heaven

0 —

1 The set up
0-30 minutes

2 Confrontation
30-90 minutes

Renowned Hollywood screen writing guru Syd Field identifies the overarching three-act format for successful screenplays as being fairly evenly split at regular timings: 30 minutes, 90 minutes and 120 minutes. Here's how it works with Frank Capra's It's A Wonderful Life (1946).

65

70

75

80

85

90

95

100

105

110

115

120

125

Potter offers George money to give up the Buildings And Loans Co.

George rejects Potter

George is racked with doubt, remembers his goal (at 15 minutes)

Voiceover tells us that Mary has 4 children & about WWII

George waves a newspaper telling of Harry's WWII medal award

Uncle Billy loses $8000 (Potter has it) – the major conflict of the story

Voiceover: present-day

Voiceover

George loses his temper and attacks Uncle Billy

George appeals to Potter to help him and is refused

George puts Zuzu's petals in his pocket

shouts at his family and has a tantrum

George runs away from his home and appears at Martini's bar

George prays for help from God

George is punched in the mouth and leaves the bar

He crashes his car into a tree and runs away

George on a bridge, Clarence (Henry Travers) appears and jumps in the river before George can

Clarence says he's an Angel

George wishes he was never born

Clarence makes his wish come true, George can hear in his deaf ear

Bedford Falls sign is changed to Pottersville

Clarence says every time a bell rings, an angels gets his wings

George discovers no-one knows him

George finds Zuzu's petals missing

George finds his home derelict

George's mother denies knowing him

Bailey Park is a graveyard, Harry is buried there, drowned aged 9

Clarence tells him 'you had a wonderful life'

Mary, a spinster librarian, runs away from George

George runs back to the bridge and prays to live again

George finds Zuzu's petals in his pocket

Reunited with his family

A miracle: money is brought to George's home by customers of the Buildings And Loans Co.

Everyone sings Hark The Herald Angels Sing

A bell on the Christmas tree rings and Zuzu says 'every time a bell rings, an angel gets their wings'

Harry arrives and tells George he's the richest man in town

End; all sing Auld Lang Syne

3 **Resolution**

90-120 minutes

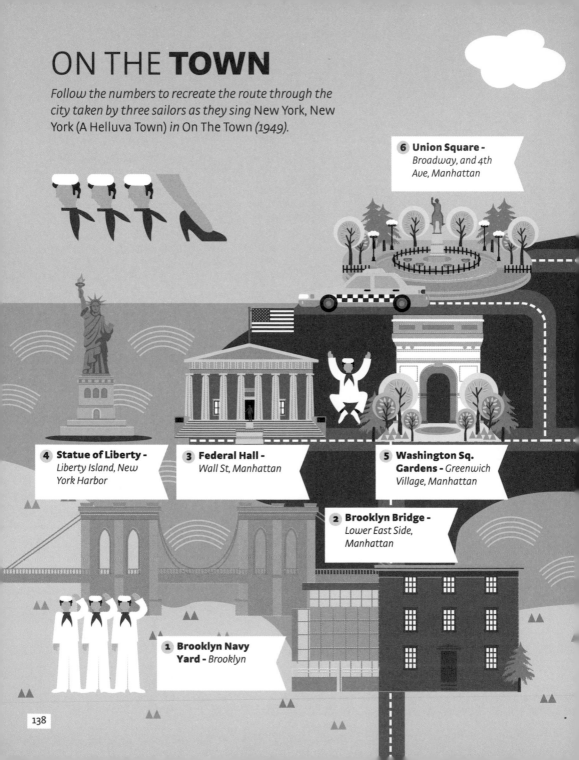

ON THE **TOWN**

Follow the numbers to recreate the route through the city taken by three sailors as they sing New York, New York (A Helluva Town) *in* On The Town *(1949).*

6 Union Square - *Broadway, and 4th Ave, Manhattan*

4 Statue of Liberty - *Liberty Island, New York Harbor*

3 Federal Hall - *Wall St, Manhattan*

5 Washington Sq. Gardens - *Greenwich Village, Manhattan*

2 Brooklyn Bridge - *Lower East Side, Manhattan*

1 Brooklyn Navy Yard - *Brooklyn*

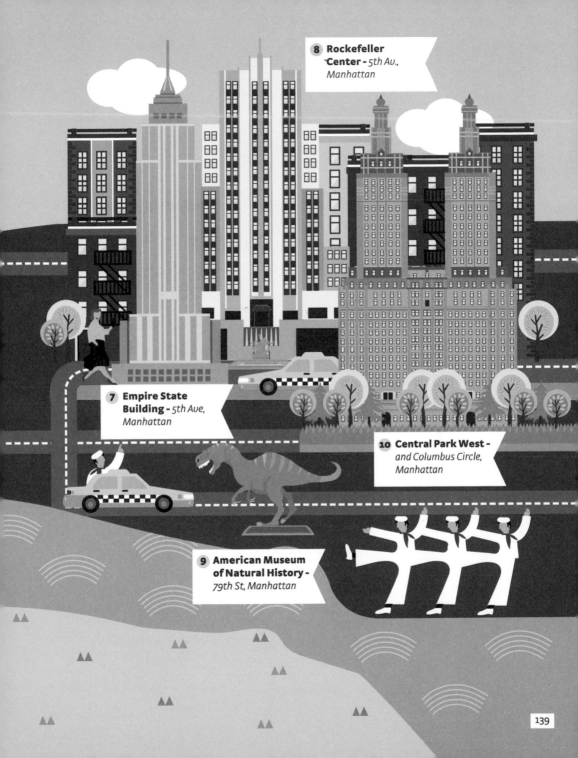

8 Rockefeller Center - 5th Av., Manhattan

7 Empire State Building - 5th Ave, Manhattan

10 Central Park West - and Columbus Circle, Manhattan

9 American Museum of Natural History - 79th St, Manhattan

NO-ONE KNOWS
ANYTHING*

Since 2005 The Black List has published top Hollywood executives' choice of the best un-filmed scripts they'd read that year. Here are the top 3 picks of each year, plus some less favoured picks that went on to become big hits.

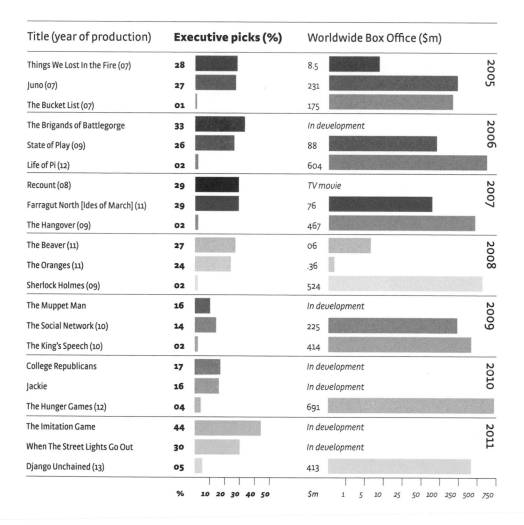

Title (year of production)	**Executive picks (%)**	Worldwide Box Office ($m)	
Things We Lost In the Fire (07)	28	8.5	2005
Juno (07)	27	231	
The Bucket List (07)	01	175	
The Brigands of Battlegorge	33	In development	2006
State of Play (09)	26	88	
Life of Pi (12)	02	604	
Recount (08)	29	TV movie	2007
Farragut North [Ides of March] (11)	29	76	
The Hangover (09)	02	467	
The Beaver (11)	27	06	2008
The Oranges (11)	24	.36	
Sherlock Holmes (09)	02	524	
The Muppet Man	16	In development	2009
The Social Network (10)	14	225	
The King's Speech (10)	02	414	
College Republicans	17	In development	2010
Jackie	16	In development	
The Hunger Games (12)	04	691	
The Imitation Game	44	In development	2011
When The Street Lights Go Out	30	In development	
Django Unchained (13)	05	413	

%   10 20 30 40 50 $m   1   5   10   25   50 100 250 500 750

 Courtesy of the Black List (http://www.blcklst.com). Additional information courtesy of Box Office Mojo and IMDb (http://www.imdb.com). Used with permission.

* William Goldman

DEAD WRITERS HAVE
ALL THE BEST STORIES

The novels by 19th century authors Jane Austen and Charles Dickens continue to engage cinema audiences. Both have had ten movies based on their work released since the millennium. Dickens' box office for the period surpasses that of Stephen King, America's most successful living author of adapted works.

KEY

- ■ Novel
- ◆ Letters
- ▲ Novella
- ● Short story
- ❶ Sense and Sensibility
- ❷ Letters of Jane Austen
- ❸ Emma
- ❹ Great Expectations

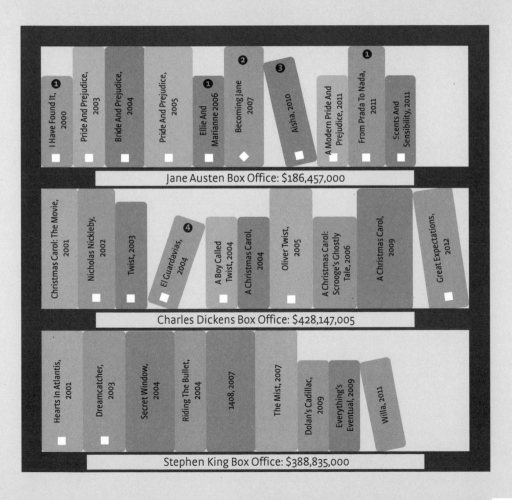

Jane Austen Box Office: $186,457,000

- ❶ I Have Found It, 2000
- Pride And Prejudice, 2003
- Bride And Prejudice, 2004
- Pride And Prejudice, 2005
- ❶ Ellie And Marianne 2006
- ❷ Becoming Jane 2007
- ❸ Aisha, 2010
- A Modern Pride And Prejudice, 2011
- ❶ From Prada To Nada, 2011
- Scents And Sensibility, 2011

Charles Dickens Box Office: $428,147,005

- Christmas Carol: The Movie, 2001
- Nicholas Nickleby, 2002
- Twist, 2003
- ❹ El Guardavias, 2004
- A Boy Called Twist, 2004
- A Christmas Carol, 2004
- Oliver Twist, 2005
- A Christmas Carol: Scrooge's Ghostly Tale, 2006
- A Christmas Carol, 2009
- Great Expectations, 2012

Stephen King Box Office: $388,835,000

- Hearts In Atlantis, 2001
- Dreamcatcher, 2003
- Secret Window, 2004
- Riding The Bullet, 2004
- 1408, 2007
- The Mist, 2007
- Dolan's Cadillac, 2009
- Everything's Eventual, 2009
- Willa, 2011

Information courtesy of IMDb (http://www.imdb.com). Used with permission.

FLIP FLOP **FILMS**

Six movies that weren't originally hits but, surprisingly, have become widely recognized masterpieces of cinema since – and successful ones too.

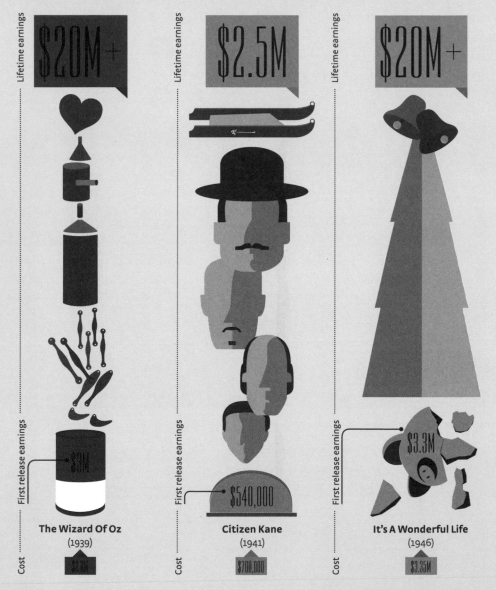

Lifetime earnings

$20M+

First release earnings

$3M

Cost

$2.3M

The Wizard Of Oz
(1939)

Lifetime earnings

$2.5M

First release earnings

$540,000

Cost

$700,000

Citizen Kane
(1941)

Lifetime earnings

$20M+

First release earnings

$3.3M

Cost

$3.3M

It's A Wonderful Life
(1946)

Lifetime earnings

$33M

First release earnings

$23.4M

Cost

Blade Runner
(1982)

$27.5M

Lifetime earnings

$46M

First release earnings

$15M

Cost

The Big Lebowski
(1998)

$15M

Lifetime earnings

$100M

First release earnings

$43M

Cost

Fight Club
(1999)

$63M

PIRATE'S **DELIGHT**

The movies most often pirated aren't always the most successful at the box office, as these 2012 figures from TorrentFreak.com, the BitTorrent-watching website, show.

DOWNLOAD RANK / TOP DOWNLOADS

1 **Project X**
(8.7m)

2 **Mission Impossible: Ghost Protocol**
(8.5m)

3 **The Dark Knight Rises**
(8.2m)

4 **The Avengers**
(8.1m)

5 **Sherlock Holmes: Game Of Shadows**
(7.85m)

6 **21 Jump Street**
(7.6m)

7 **The Girl With The Dragon Tattoo**
(7.4m)

8 **The Dictator**
(7.3m)

9 **Ice Age: Continental Drift**
(6.9m)

10 **Twilight Saga Breaking Dawn Part 1**
(6.7m)

Shark-infested waters

Shark-infested waters

STUDIO COAST

Calm waters

TOP BOX OFFICE / BOX OFFICE RANK

The Avengers
($1.5bn) 1

The Dark Knight Rises
($1.1bn) 2

Ice Age: Continental Drift
($875m) 3

Twilight Saga Breaking Dawn Part 1
($712m) 4

Mission Impossible: Ghost Protocol
($694m) 5

Sherlock Holmes: Game Of Shadows
($544m) 6

The Girl With The Dragon Tattoo
($233m) 7

21 Jump Street
($202m) 8

The Dictator
($178m) 9

Project X
($101m) 10

Calm waters

Most Pirated movies of all time (2006 to August 2012, source: TorrentFreak.com).
Additional information courtesy of Box Office Mojo and IMDb (http://www.imdb.com). Used with permission.

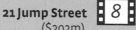

145

ANY **RESEMBLANCE**?

What is it about serial killers that moviemakers find so interesting?
Given the figures here, there is no clear correlation between the
number of victims and the number of movies made about the killer.

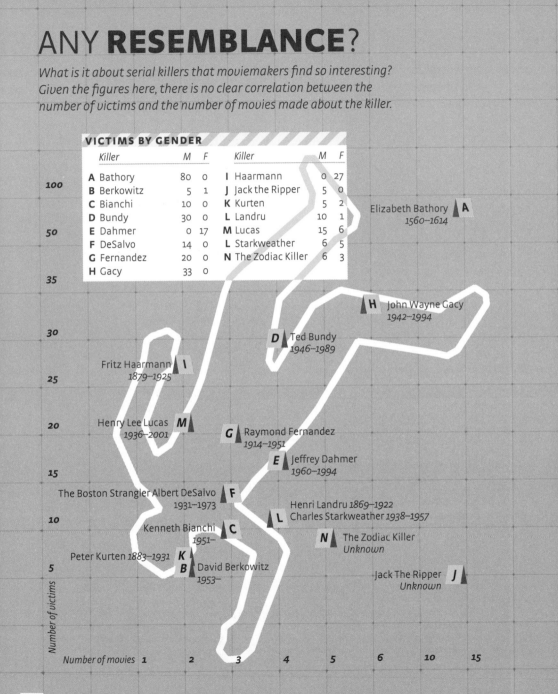

VICTIMS BY GENDER

Killer	M	F	Killer	M	F
A Bathory	80	0	**I** Haarmann	0	27
B Berkowitz	5	1	**J** Jack the Ripper	5	0
C Bianchi	10	0	**K** Kurten	5	2
D Bundy	30	0	**L** Landru	10	1
E Dahmer	0	17	**M** Lucas	15	6
F DeSalvo	14	0	**L** Starkweather	6	5
G Fernandez	20	0	**N** The Zodiac Killer	6	3
H Gacy	33	0			

Elizabeth Bathory **A**
1560–1614

John Wayne Gacy **H**
1942–1994

Ted Bundy **D**
1946–1989

Fritz Haarmann **I**
1879–1925

Henry Lee Lucas **M**
1936–2001

Raymond Fernandez **G**
1914–1951

Jeffrey Dahmer **E**
1960–1994

The Boston Strangler Albert DeSalvo **F**
1931–1973

Henri Landru *1869–1922*
Charles Starkweather *1938–1957* **L**

Kenneth Bianchi **C**
1951–

The Zodiac Killer **N**
Unknown

Peter Kurten *1883–1931* **K**

David Berkowitz **B**
1953–

Jack The Ripper **J**
Unknown

Number of victims

100   50   35   30   25   20   15   10   5

Number of movies   1   2   3   4   5   6   10   15

Additional information courtesy of IMDb (http://www.imdb.com). Used with permission.

TOM HANKS **THANKS**

*The actor with the biggest box office success in America likes to work
with directors he knows, and they like working with him.*

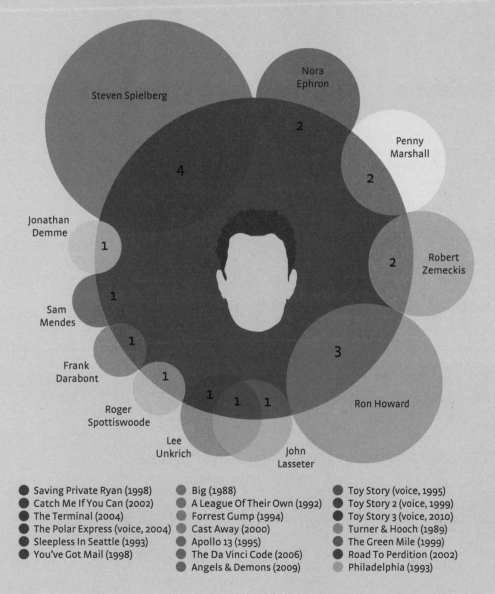

Steven Spielberg

Nora Ephron

2

Penny Marshall

4

2

Jonathan Demme

1

Robert Zemeckis

1

2

Sam Mendes

1

Frank Darabont

1

3

Roger Spottiswoode

1   1   1

Ron Howard

Lee Unkrich

John Lasseter

- ● Saving Private Ryan (1998)
- ● Catch Me If You Can (2002)
- ● The Terminal (2004)
- ● The Polar Express (voice, 2004)
- ● Sleepless In Seattle (1993)
- ● You've Got Mail (1998)

- ● Big (1988)
- ● A League Of Their Own (1992)
- ● Forrest Gump (1994)
- ● Cast Away (2000)
- ● Apollo 13 (1995)
- ● The Da Vinci Code (2006)
- ● Angels & Demons (2009)

- ● Toy Story (voice, 1995)
- ● Toy Story 2 (voice, 1999)
- ● Toy Story 3 (voice, 2010)
- ● Turner & Hooch (1989)
- ● The Green Mile (1999)
- ● Road To Perdition (2002)
- ● Philadelphia (1993)

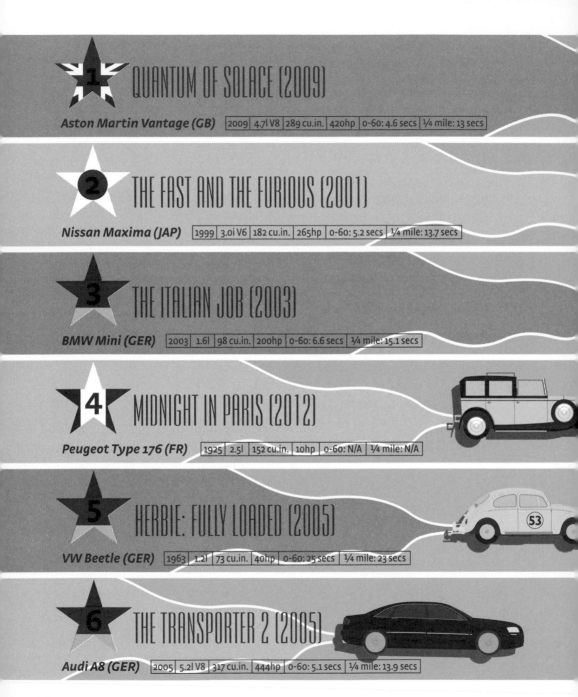

1 QUANTUM OF SOLACE (2009)

Aston Martin Vantage (GB) | 2009 | 4.7l V8 | 289 cu.in. | 420hp | 0-60: 4.6 secs | ¼ mile: 13 secs

2 THE FAST AND THE FURIOUS (2001)

Nissan Maxima (JAP) | 1999 | 3.0i V6 | 182 cu.in. | 265hp | 0-60: 5.2 secs | ¼ mile: 13.7 secs

3 THE ITALIAN JOB (2003)

BMW Mini (GER) | 2003 | 1.6l | 98 cu.in. | 200hp | 0-60: 6.6 secs | ¼ mile: 15.1 secs

4 MIDNIGHT IN PARIS (2012)

Peugeot Type 176 (FR) | 1925 | 2.5l | 152 cu.in. | 10hp | 0-60: N/A | ¼ mile: N/A

5 HERBIE: FULLY LOADED (2005)

VW Beetle (GER) | 1963 | 1.2l | 73 cu.in. | 40hp | 0-60: 25 secs | ¼ mile: 23 secs

6 THE TRANSPORTER 2 (2005)

Audi A8 (GER) | 2005 | 5.2l V8 | 317 cu.in. | 444hp | 0-60: 5.1 secs | ¼ mile: 13.9 secs

Top Speed
180mph
290kph

Gross
$586m

Top Speed
150mph
241kph

Gross
$207m

Top Speed
134mph
216kph

Gross
$176m

THE IMPORT
GETAWAY

Not all cars are American, just as not all movies are American. The following cars from around the world starred in these successful movies. While we could have chosen any Bond movie to illustrate the worth of the Aston Martin, the one featured here contains the best chase scenes of the 21st-century Bond movies.

Top Speed
68mph
109kph

Gross
$151m

Top Speed
83mph
134kph

Gross
$144m

Top Speed
155mph
249kph

Gross
$85m

GOLDEN BEARS AND LIONS

The oldest international film festivals are those held at Venice, Italy (established 1932), Cannes, France (est. 1947), and Berlin, Germany (est. 1951). All of them make a top award to the year's best international movie. The results give us a clue as to which nationalities like their neighbours' movies most: no Spanish films have won a Golden Lion, for instance, but seven German movies have.

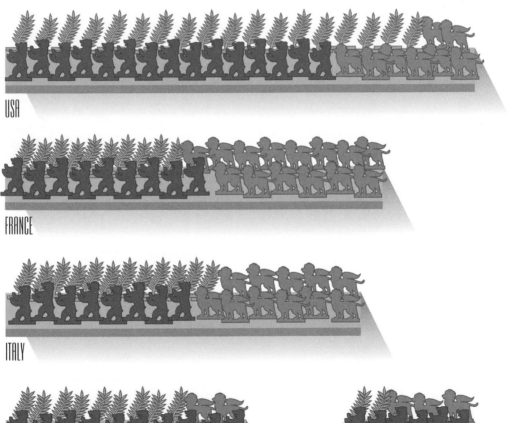

USA

FRANCE

ITALY

UK

WEST GERMANY

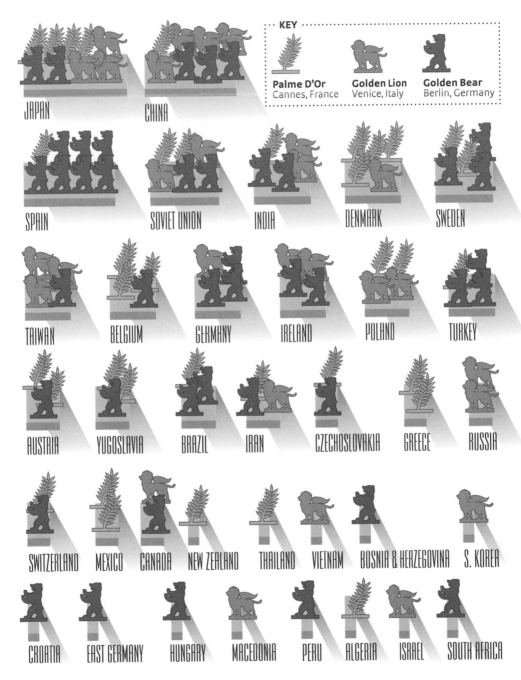

KEY

Palme D'Or
Cannes, France

Golden Lion
Venice, Italy

Golden Bear
Berlin, Germany

JAPAN

CHINA

SPAIN

SOVIET UNION

INDIA

DENMARK

SWEDEN

TAIWAN

BELGIUM

GERMANY

IRELAND

POLAND

TURKEY

AUSTRIA

YUGOSLAVIA

BRAZIL

IRAN

CZECHOSLOVAKIA

GREECE

RUSSIA

SWITZERLAND

MEXICO

CANADA

NEW ZEALAND

THAILAND

VIETNAM

BOSNIA & HERZEGOVINA

S. KOREA

CROATIA

EAST GERMANY

HUNGARY

MACEDONIA

PERU

ALGERIA

ISRAEL

SOUTH AFRICA

NEVER WORK **WITH KIDS**?

Who's the Daddy or Mommy? These four actors have appeared in movies alongside more children than anyone else in recent movie history.

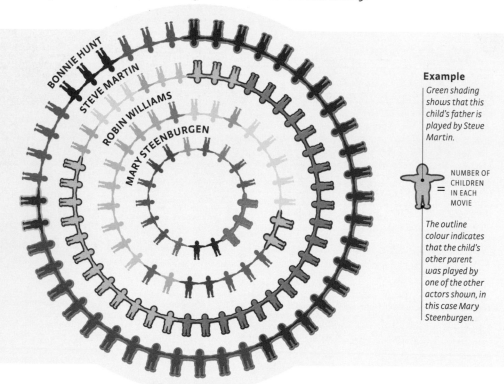

Example

Green shading shows that this child's father is played by Steve Martin.

NUMBER OF CHILDREN IN EACH MOVIE

The outline colour indicates that the child's other parent was played by one of the other actors shown, in this case Mary Steenburgen.

BONNIE HUNT
- Beethoven
- Beethoven's 2nd
- Now And Then
- Jumanji
- Cheaper By The Dozen
- Cheaper By The Dozen 2

STEVE MARTIN
- Parenthood
- Father Of The Bride
- A Simple Twist of Fate
- Father Of The Bride Part II
- Bringing Down The House
- Cheaper By The Dozen
- Cheaper By The Dozen 2

ROBIN WILLIAMS
- Mrs Doubtfire
- Jumanji
- Jack
- Father's Day
- What Dreams May Come
- Jakob The Liar
- Bicentennial Man
- RV: Runaway Vacation
- The Night Listener
- August Rush
- World's Greatest Dad
- Old Dogs

MARY STEENBURGEN
- One Magic Christmas
- Parenthood
- It Runs In The Family
- Powder
- I Am Sam
- Sunshine State
- Elf
- Step Brothers
- In The Electric Mist

THERE WILL BE **BLOOD**

The slasher sub-genre of horror movies began in the 1970s and spawned a host of killers who stabbed, strangled, shot and decapitated their teenage victims for the next five decades. But who killed more people, and in which decade did most blood flow?

Legend:
- The Texas Chainsaw Massacre
- Halloween
- Friday The 13th
- A Nightmare On Elm Street
- Scream
- Saw

1970s
TOTAL VICTIMS **10**
- 1 film — 5 victims
- 1 film — 5 victims

1980s
TOTAL VICTIMS **224**
- 1 film — 8 victims
- 4 films — 69 victims
- 8 films — 116 victims
- 5 films — 31 victims

1990s
TOTAL VICTIMS **127**
- 2 films — 19 victims
- 3 films — 52 victims
- 1 film — 25 victims
- 1 film — 8 victims
- 1 film — 10 victims

2000s
TOTAL VICTIMS **154**
- 2 films — 17 victims
- 2 films — 22 victims
- 1 film — 21 victims
- 2 films — 21 victims
- 2 films — 18 victims
- 6 films — 54 victims

2010s
TOTAL VICTIMS **45**
- 1 film — 5 victims
- 1 film — 13 victims
- 1 film — 27 victims

- **Jason** 162 kills in 10 movies = average **16.2** kills per movie
- **Michael Myers** 148 kills in 10 movies = **14.8** kills
- **Jigsaw** (+ apprentices) 81 kills in 7 movies = **11.5** kills
- **Ghostface** 41 kills in 4 movies = **10.25** kills
- **Leatherface** 49 kills in 6 movies = **8.1** kills
- **Freddy** 65 kills in 9 movies = **7.2** kills

WHO'S
LAUGHING?

*Identify these famous comedies.
The first letter of the title is included
to help you identify each one.*

THE **PERFECT** DATE MOVIE

Or ten things I love about you!
The mixed ingredients for a
perfect rom-com date movie.

Movie titles (arranged in petals):

HE'S JUST NOT THAT INTO YOU (2009)
CONFESSIONS OF A SHOPAHOLIC (2009)
THE TIME TRAVELLER'S WIFE (2009)
NOW AND FOREVER (2002)
WHAT HAPPENS IN VEGAS (2008)
MISS CONGENIALITY (2000)
REEL LOVE (2011)
MUST LOVE DOGS (2005)
THE HOLIDAY (2006)
MADE OF HONOR (2008)

THE MIRROR HAS TWO FACES (1996)
THE SWEET HOME ALABAMA (2002)
THE TRUTH ABOUT CATS AND DOGS (1996)
BRIDGET JONES'S DIARY (2001)
WHEN HARRY MET SALLY (1989)
FOUR WEDDINGS AND A FUNERAL (1994)
PRETTY WOMAN (1990)
KATE AND LEOPOLD (2001)
GHOST (1990)
PRETTY IN PINK (1986)

27 DRESSES (2008)
SEX AND THE CITY (2007)
WHILE YOU WERE SLEEPING (1995)
THE LAKE HOUSE (2006)
SHE'S ALL THAT (1999)
YOU'VE GOT MAIL (1998)
DAVID FRANKEL'S THE DEVIL WEARS PRADA (2006)
ONE FINE DAY (1996)
...-UP (2006)
...BREAK...NATION (2010)

HOW TO LOSE A GUY IN 10 DAYS (2003)
AS GOOD AS IT GETS (1997)
NEW IN TOWN (2009)
NEVER BEEN KISSED (1999)
THE 40-YEAR-OLD VIRGIN (2005)
TRULY, MADLY, DEEPLY (1990)
THE BUTTERFLY EFFECT (2004)
THE SWEETEST THING (2002)
THE WEDDING PLANNER (2001)
10 THINGS I HATE ABOUT YOU (1995)

Storylines

1. They're a perfect match... eventually
2. She's a sad loveless writer
3. Man and woman are brought together by dogs
4. The city girl finds love in a small town
5. She's gorgeous but doesn't think so
6. Bad influences get in the way
7. She's in love with a dead guy
8. They Can Hold Back Time (kinda)
9. Love comes with matching hats and shoes
10. Always the bridesmaid... until she meets him

Actresses

JENNIFER ANISTON	HELEN HUNT	LEEANN RIMES
DREW BARRYMORE	CATHERINE KEENER	MOLLY RINGWALD
SANDRA BULLOCK	MIA KIRSHNER	JULIA ROBERTS
RACHAEL LEIGH COOK	DIANE LANE	MEG RYAN
KAT DENNINGS	JENNIFER LOPEZ	AMY SMART
CAMERON DIAZ	ANDIE MCDOWELL	JULIET STEPHENSON
ISLA FISHER	MICHELLE MONAGHAN	JULIA STILES
JANEANE GAROFALO	DEMI MOORE	BARBRA STREISAND
ANNE HATHAWAY	SARAH JESSICA PARKER	KATE WINSLET
KATHERINE HEIGL	MICHELLE PFEIFFER	REESE WITHERSPOON
KATE HUDSON	RACHEL MCADAMS	RENEE ZELLWEGGER

DANIEL DAY LEWIS:
HAIR APPARENT

*Each of the three roles for which Daniel Day Lewis has won an Oscar
have required he grow lots of facial hair. When clean shaven on screen
he invariably loses top awards to men who have more facial hair.*

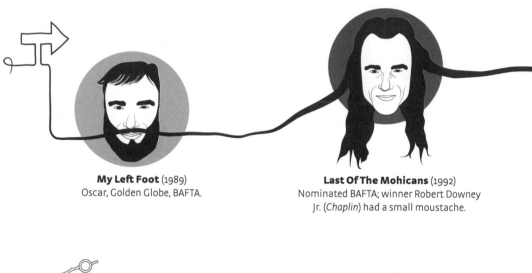

My Left Foot (1989)
Oscar, Golden Globe, BAFTA.

Last Of The Mohicans (1992)
Nominated BAFTA; winner Robert Downey
Jr. (*Chaplin*) had a small moustache.

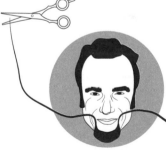

Lincoln (2012)
Golden Globe, Oscar, BAFTA.

Nine (2009)
Nominated Golden Globe Best Actor
in a Comedy or Musical; winner Robert
Downey Jr. (*Sherlock Holmes*) had
stubble/five o'clock shadow.

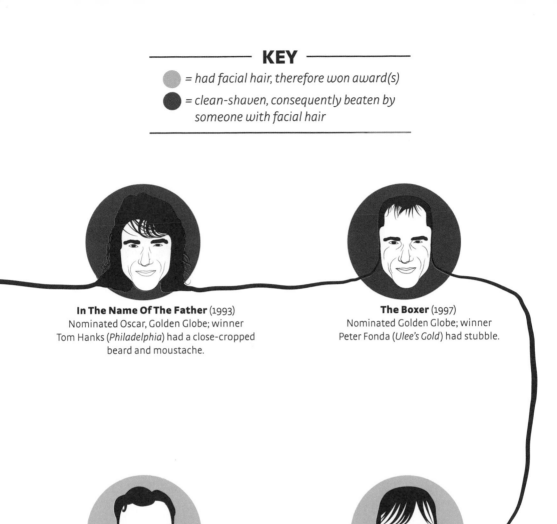

In The Name Of The Father (1993)
Nominated Oscar, Golden Globe; winner Tom Hanks (*Philadelphia*) had a close-cropped beard and moustache.

The Boxer (1997)
Nominated Golden Globe; winner Peter Fonda (*Ulee's Gold*) had stubble.

There Will Be Blood (2007)
Oscar, Golden Globe, BAFTA.

Gangs Of New York (2002)
BAFTA. Nominated Oscar; winner Adrien Brody (*The Pianist*), had a full beard and moustache. Nominated Golden Globe; winner Jack Nicholson (*About Schmidt*) had significant stubble.

END GAMES

The top most successful apocalyptic movies have shown the world facing disaster and the human race extinction via four main sources — God, Man, Mother Nature and Outer Space.

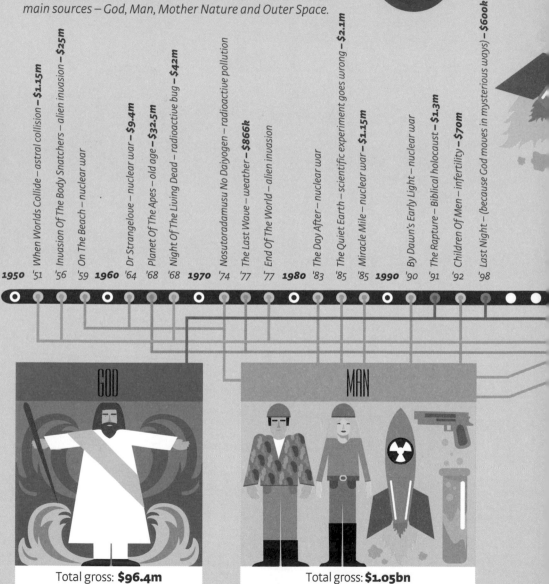

When Worlds Collide – astral collision – **$1.15m**
Invasion Of The Body Snatchers – alien invasion – **$25m**
On The Beach – nuclear war
Dr Strangelove – nuclear war – **$9.4m**
Planet Of The Apes – old age – **$32.5m**
Night Of The Living Dead – radioactive bug – **$42m**
Nosutoradamusu No Daiyogen – radioactive pollution
The Last Wave – weather – **$866k**
End Of The World – alien invasion
The Day After – nuclear war
The Quiet Earth – scientific experiment goes wrong – **$2.1m**
Miracle Mile – nuclear war – **$1.15m**
By Dawn's Early Light – nuclear war
The Rapture – Biblical holocaust – **$1.3m**
Children Of Men – infertility – **$70m**
Last Night – (because God moves in mysterious ways) – **$600k**

| 1950 | '51 | '56 | '59 | 1960 | '64 | '68 | '68 | 1970 | '74 | '77 | '77 | 1980 | '83 | '85 | '85 | 1990 | '90 | '91 | '92 | '98 |

GOD

Total gross: **$96.4m**

MAN

Total gross: **$1.05bn**

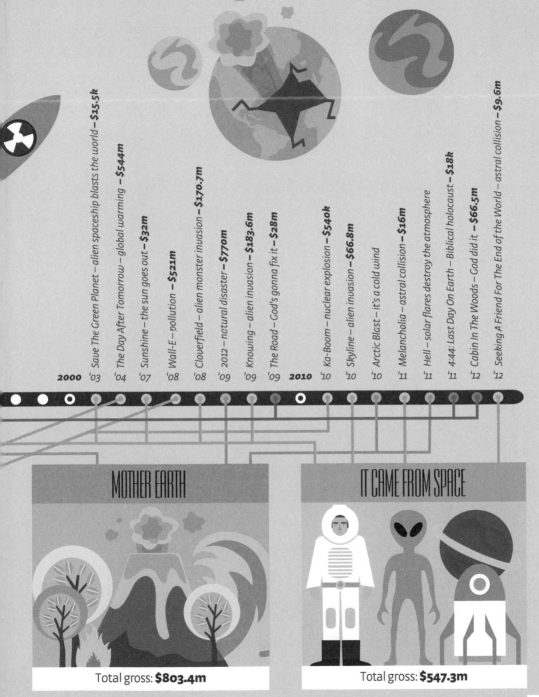

Save The Green Planet – alien spaceship blasts the world – **$15.5k**

The Day After Tomorrow – global warming – **$544m**

Sunshine – the sun goes out – **$32m**

Wall-E – pollution – **$521m**

Cloverfield – alien monster invasion – **$170.7m**

2012 – natural disaster – **$770m**

Knowing – alien invasion – **$183.6m**

The Road – God's gonna fix it – **$28m**

Ka-Boom – nuclear explosion – **$540k**

Skyline – alien invasion – **$66.8m**

Arctic Blast – it's a cold wind

Melancholia – astral collision – **$16m**

Hell – solar flares destroy the atmosphere

4:44: Last Day On Earth – Biblical holocaust – **$18k**

Cabin In The Woods – God did it – **$66.5m**

Seeking A Friend For The End of the World – astral collision – **$9.6m**

2000 '03 '04 '07 '08 '08 '09 '09 '09 **2010** '10 '10 '10 '11 '11 '11 '12 '12

MOTHER EARTH

Total gross: **$803.4m**

IT CAME FROM SPACE

Total gross: **$547.3m**

Information courtesy of Box Office Mojo. Used with permission.

Credits

Produced by Essential Works Ltd
essentialworks.co.uk

Essential Works

Art Director: Michael Gray
Supervising Editor:
Johnny Morgan
Editors: Nicola Hodgson,
Fiona Screen
Layout: Gemma Wilson

Octopus

Editorial Director:
Trevor Davies
Senior Production Manager:
Peter Hunt

Designers

Marc Morera Agustí (62-3)
Lizzie Astles (24-5)
Jake Bartok (38-9)
Stef Bayley (13, 31, 58-9, 133)
Antony Bearpark (48)
Federica Bonfanti (22-3, 44-5)
Marwa Boukarim (150-1)
Giulia De Amicis (102-3)
Barbara Doherty (28-9, 46-7,
    81, 87, 116, 135, 153)
Cruz Dragosavac (72-3)
Jacopo Ferretti (26-7, 40-1, 114-5)
Clarissa Gonzalez (61)
Lorena Guerra (49, 64-5, 80, 82-3,
    88-9, 92, 108, 109, 120, 141)
Simon Heard (11)
Natasha Hellegouarch (32-3,
    90-1, 96, 122, 138, 158)
Daniel Nolen (69)
Sam Parij (14-5, 94-5, 156-7)

Saakshita Prabhakar (36-7, 134)
Darren Reynolds (16-7, 42-3, 70-1,
    140, 144-5, 146, 148-9)
Matteo Riva (54-5, 66-7, 100-1,
    128-9, 130-1)
Aleksandar Savic (78, 104, 117)
Yael Shinkar (20, 84-5, 126-7,
    142-3)
Shahed Syed (50-1)
Cristina Vanko (76-7)
Mengying Wang (56)
Ryan Welch (21, 68, 93)
James Wendelborn (57)
Stephen Wildish (12, 34, 79, 98,
    132, 154)
Scott Williams (112-3)
Gemma Wilson (18-9, 52, 53, 105,
    110-1, 121, 147, 152)
Anil Yanik (74-5)

Guess the film answers

1970s (page 12)
The Poseidon Adventure; X, Y And Zee; Jaws; Rocky;
Yanks; Apocalypse Now; One Flew Over The
Cuckoo's Nest; Deliverance; Herbie Rides Again;
Westworld

1980s (page 34)
Flight Of The Navigator; Teen Wolf; The
Untouchables; Zelig; Labyrinth; Dirty Dancing;
Honey, I Shrunk The Kids; Xanadu; Back To The
Future; The Princess Bride

1990s (page 79)
Outbreak; Ghost; You've Got Mail; The X-Files;
Dumb & Dumber; Look Who's Talking; Home Alone;
Quiz Show; The Usual Suspects; The Bodyguard

2000s (page 98)
V For Vendetta; Brokeback Mountain; Eternal
Sunshine Of The Spotless Mind; Napoleon
Dynamite; O Brother Where Art Thou?; Gangs Of
New York; Road To Perdition; Y Tu Mamá También;
Unbreakable; Amélie

Adaptations (page 132)
The Lovely Bones; The Shining; Charlie And The
Chocolate Factory; True Grit; We Need To Talk
About Kevin; The French Lieutenant's Woman; No
Country For Old Men; Zodiac; American Psycho;
The Hound Of The Baskervilles; Indecent Proposal;
Young Adam; The Day Of The Jackal; Ulysses;
Breakfast At Tiffany's; K-Pax; The English Patient;
The Remains Of The Day; Vanity Fair; The Girl With
The Dragon Tattoo

Comedy (page 154)
Happy Gilmore; Kingpin; Spaceballs; Dr
Strangelove; Vice Versa; Uncle Buck; Quick Change;
Carry On Doctor; Old School; The Pink Panther;
Groundhog Day; Napoleon Dynamite; The Jerk; Four
Lions; Meet The Fokkers; Roxanne; Best In Show;
Young Frankenstein; Withnail And I; Life of Brian